Teaching Creation Science in Public Schools

By

Duane T. Gish, Ph.D.

Teaching Creation Science in Public Schools
Duane T. Gish

Copyright © 1995

Institute for Creation Research
P.O. Box 2667
El Cajon, California 92021

Library of Congress Catalog Card Number:
ISBN 0–932766–36–6

Cataloging in Publication Data

Printed in the United States of America

About the Author . . .

Dr. Gish received a B.S. degree from the University of California at Los Angeles with a major in Chemistry, and a Ph.D. degree from the University of California at Berkeley with a major in biochemistry. He spent a total of 18 years in biochemical research; with three years at Cornell University Medical College, New York City, four years with the Virus Laboratory, University of California, Berkeley, and eleven years on the research staff of The Upjohn Company, a pharmaceutical firm, Kalamazoo, Michigan. During that time, Dr. Gish worked with two Nobel Prize winners.

In 1971, Dr. Gish left his position with The Upjohn Company to join Dr. Henry Morris in his present work with the Institute for Creation Research, where he serves as Senior Vice President. He has published approximately forty technical articles in scientific journals. He is the author of numerous articles and several books on the subject of the scientific evidence for creation. He has participated in nearly 300 debates and has lectured in 49 of the 50 states, in most provinces of Canada, and in about 35 foreign countries. He is a member of the American Chemical Society and is a Fellow of the American Institute of Chemists. He is one of the founders and a board member of the Creation Research Society.

Table of Contents

Preface

The question of origins is a subject that extends far beyond the biological and physical sciences. Theories in the behavioral sciences, political and economic theories, and more particularly one's philosophy and religion, are profoundly influenced by one's view of origins. In our pluralistic democratic nation that cherishes academic and religious freedoms, it is thus especially important that no theory of origins be allowed to freeze into dogma while its advocates permit no alternative theories or exposure of its weaknesses and fallacies. This is now the situation, however, that dominates the scientific and educational establishments throughout the United States.

During the Scopes Trial in 1925, when the Tennessee law that excluded the teaching of the theory of evolution was being challenged, Clarence Darrow thundered that it was bigotry to teach only one theory of origins. We are now about 70 years after the Scopes Trial, and the situation has been essentially turned around 180 degrees. Evolutionists are insisting that evolution be taught as a fact in our tax-supported public schools, and they are resorting to every means possible to exclude the teaching of the scientific evidence that supports creation. Just as the discredited Lamarckian genetics was at one time the exclusive state-approved theory of genetics that was taught in the schools, colleges and universities of the Soviet Union, so has the theory of evolution become the unofficial, state-sanctioned theory of origins that is taught in the textbooks and classrooms of American public schools.

Although they constitute a minority, there are thousands of scientists in the U.S. today who have become convinced that the theory of evolution is scientifically untenable and that the theory of creation offers a far superior scientific model for correlating and explaining the evidence related to origins. In the accompanying booklet are set forth the scientific, pedagogical, and philosophical reasons for teaching the scientific evidence that supports creation along with the evidence evolutionists believe supports evolution.

We believe, along with Darrow, that to teach only one theory of origins is bigotry. Furthermore, it is bad science, bad education and a violation of the academic and religious freedoms of both teachers and students. This unfortunate situation can only be remedied by teaching both theories of origins in a philosophically neutral manner excluding the use of all religious literature, including the literature of religions based on evolution (humanism, atheism, pantheism, etc.).

Chapter One

The Nature of Science and of Theories on Origins

The Nature of Science and of Scientific Theories

Science is our attempt to observe, understand and explain the operation of the universe and of the living things found here on planet Earth. Since a scientific theory, by definition, must be testable by repeatable observations and must be capable of being falsified if indeed it were false, a scientific theory can only attempt to explain processes and events that are presently occurring repeatedly within our observations. Theories about history, although interesting and often fruitful, are not scientific theories, even though they may be related to other theories which do fulfill the criteria of a scientific theory. While operating within the domain of empirical science, creation scientists function in exactly the same manner as evolution scientists, assuming that what they see happening today happened in the past and will happen in the same way in the future. Science is empirical, and thus this is the only way a scientist can operate.

The Nature of Theories on Origins

On the other hand, the theory of creation and the theory of evolution are attempts to explain the origin of the universe and of its inhabitants. There were no human observers to the origin of the universe, the origin of life, or as a matter of fact, to the origin of a single living species. These events were unique historical events which have occurred only once. Thus, no one has ever seen anything created, nor has anyone ever seen a fish evolve into an amphibian nor an ape evolve into man. Furthermore, it is impossible to go into the laboratory and test any theory on how a fish may have changed into an amphibian or how an ape-like creature may have evolved into man. The changes we see occurring today are mere fluctuations in populations which result neither in an increase in complexity nor significant change. Therefore, neither creation nor evolution is a scientific theory. Creation and evolution are inferences based on circumstantial evidence.

Thus the notion, repeated incessantly by evolutionists, that evolution is a scientific theory while creation is nothing more than religious mysticism is blatantly false. This is being recognized more and more today, even by evolutionists themselves. Karl Popper, one of the world's leading philosophers of science, has stated that evolution is not a scientific theory but is a metaphysical research program.[1] Birch and Ehrlich state that:

> Our theory of evolution has become . . . one which cannot be refuted by any possible observation. Every conceivable observation can be fitted into it. It is thus "outside of empirical science" but not necessarily false. No one can think of ways in which to test it. Ideas, either without basis or based on a few laboratory experiments carried out in extremely simplified systems have attained currency far beyond their validity. They have become part of an evolutionary dogma accepted by most of us as part of our training.[2]

Green and Goldberger, with reference to theories on the origin of life, have said that:

> . . . the macromolecule-to-cell transition is a jump of fantastic dimensions, which lies beyond the range of testable hypothesis. In this area all is conjecture.[3]

It seems obvious that a theory that is outside of empirical science because no one can think of ways to test it, or a theory that lies beyond the range of

---

[1] Karl Popper, in *The Philosophy of Karl Popper*, ed. P. A. Schilpp, Vol. 1 (La Salle, IL: Open Court), pp 133-143.

[2] L. C. Birch and P. R. Ehrlich, *Nature* 214 (1967): 369.

[3] D. E. Green and R. F. Goldberger, *Molecular Insights into the Living Process* (New York: Academic Press, 1967), p. 407.

testable hypothesis, cannot qualify as a scientific theory. Any suggestion that these challenges to the status of evolution as a scientific theory are exceptions lifted out of the evolutionary literature by creation scientists can be refuted by a thorough search of that literature. Even Futuyma, one of those who has recently written a book attempting to refute creation, states in that book that:

> Two major kinds of arguments about evolutionary theory occur within scientific circles. There are philosophical arguments about whether or not evolutionary theory qualifies as a scientific theory, and substantive arguments about the details of the theory and their adequacy to explain observed phenomena. . . . A secondary issue then arises: Is the hypothesis of natural selection falsifiable or is it a tautology? . . . The claim that natural selection is a tautology is periodically made in the scientific literature itself. . . ."[4]

It is evident that the major challenge to the status of evolution as a scientific theory comes from within the evolutionary establishment itself, not from creation scientists.

Creation and evolution are thus theoretical inferences about history. Even though neither qualifies, strictly speaking, as a scientific theory, each possesses scientific character, since each attempts to correlate and explain scientific data. Creation and evolution are best characterized as explanatory scientific models which are employed to correlate and explain data related to origins. The terms "creation theory," "evolution theory," "creation science" and "evolution science" are appropriate as long as it is clear that the use of such terms denote certain inferences about the history of origins which employ scientific data rather than referring to testable and potentially falsifiable scientific theories. Since neither is a scientific theory and each seeks to explain the same scientific data related to origins, it is not only incorrect but arrogant and self-serving to declare that evolution is science while creation is mere religion. Creation is in every sense as scientific as evolution.

---

[4] D. J. Futuyma, *Science on Trial* (New York: Pantheon Books, 1983), p. 171.

The Relationship of Theories on Origins To Philosophy and Religion

No theory on origins can be devoid of philosophical and religious implications. Creation implies the existence of a Creator (a person or persons, a force, an intelligence, or whatever one may wish to impute). The creation scientist assumes that the natural universe is the product of the design, purpose and direct volitional acts of a Creator. Science can tell us nothing about who the Creator is, why the universe was created, or anything about the relationship of the things created to the Creator. Creation scientists have no intention of introducing religious literature into science classes or science textbooks in the public schools of the United States. It is thus absolutely untrue to say that creation scientists are seeking to introduce Biblical creation into the public schools. Their desire is that the subject of origins be taught in a philosophically and religiously neutral manner, as required by the U.S. Constitution.

On the other hand, evolution is a non-theistic theory of origins which by definition excludes the intervention of an outside agency of any kind. Evolutionists believe that by employing natural laws and processes *plus nothing* it is possible to explain the origin of the universe and of all that it contains. This involves the acceptance of a particular philosophical or metaphysical world view and is thus basically religious in nature. The fact that creation and evolution involve fundamentally different world views has been frankly admitted by some evolutionists. For example, Lewontin has said:

> Yet, whatever our understanding of the social struggle that gives rise to creationism, whatever the desire to reconcile science and religion may be, there is no escape from the fundamental contradiction between evolution and creationism. They are irreconcilable world views.[5]

Thus, Lewontin characterizes creation and evolution as *irreconcilable world views*, and as such each involves commitment to irreconcilable philosophical and religious positions. This does not imply that all evolutionists are atheists or agnostics, nor does it imply that all creationists are Bible-believing fundamentalists.

---

[5] R. Lewontin, in the Introduction to *Scientists Confront Creationism*, ed. L. R. Godfrey (New York: W.W. Norton and Co., 1983), p. xxvi.

While it is true that teaching creation science exclusively would en-
courage belief in a theistic world-view, it is equally true that teaching evolution science exclusively (as is essentially the case in the U.S. today)
encourages belief in a non-theistic, and in fact, an essentially atheistic, world
view. Indoctrinating our young people in evolutionism tends to convince
them that they are hardly more than a mechanistic product of a mindless universe, that there is no God, that there is no one to whom they are responsible.
Thus, Julian Huxley asserted that:

> Darwinism removed the whole idea of God as
> the creator of organisms from the sphere of ra-
> tional discussion . . . we can dismiss entirely all
> ideas of a supernatural overriding mind being re-
> sponsible for the evolutionary process.[6]

In their literature, humanists have proclaimed that humanism is a
"non-theistic religion." They quote Sir Julian Huxley as stating:

> I use the word "Humanist" to mean someone
> who believes that man is just as much a natural
> phenomenon as an animal or plant; that his body,
> mind and soul were not supernaturally created but
> are products of evolution. . . .[7]

In his review of George Gaylord Simpson's book *Life of the Past*,[8] Huxley
says:

> And he concludes the book with a splendid as-
> sertion of the evolutionists' view of man. Man, he
> writes, "stands alone in the universe, a unique
> product of a long, unconscious, impersonal, mate-
> rial process. . . . He can and must decide and
> manage his own destiny."[9]

---

[6] J. Huxley, in *Issues in Evolution,* ed. S. Tax (Chicago: University of
Chicago Press, 1960), p. 45.
[7] "What is Humanism?" Humanist Community of San Jose (San Jose,
CA 95106).
[8] G. G. Simpson, *Life of the Past* (New Haven, Conn.: Yale
University Press, 1953), p. 157.
[9] J. Huxley, *Scientific American*, 189 (1953): 90.

In his eulogy to Theodosius Dobzhansky, one of the world's leading evolutionists until his death, Ayala wrote that:

> . . . Dobzhansky believed and propounded that the implications of biological evolution reach much beyond biology into philosophy, sociology, and even socio-political issues. The place of biological evolution in human thought was, according to Dobzhansky, best expressed in a passage he often quoted from Pierre Teilhard de Chardin: "(Evolution) is a general postulate to which all theories, all hypotheses, all systems must henceforward bow and which they must satisfy in order to be thinkable and true. Evolution is a light which illuminates all facts, a trajectory which all lines of thought must follow—this is what evolution is."[10]

The above statement is as heavily saturated with religion as any assertion could be, and yet it is quoted approvingly by Ayala and Dobzhansky, two of the main architects of the neo-Darwinian theory of evolution.

It is no wonder that Marjorie Grene, a leading philosopher and historian of science, has stated that:

> It is as a *religion of science* that Darwinism chiefly held, and holds men's minds. The derivation of life, of man, of man's deepest hopes and highest achievements, from the external and indirect determination of small chance errors, appears as the very keystone of the naturalistic universe. . . . Today the tables are turned. The modified, but still characteristically Darwinian theory has itself become an orthodoxy preached by its adherents with religious fervor, and doubted, they feel, only by a few muddlers imperfect in scientific faith.[11]

Birch and Ehrlich have used the term "evolutionary dogma," Grene has referred to Darwinism as a "religion of science," an "orthodoxy preached by its adherents with religious fervor," and Dobzhansky and Teilhard de

---

[10] F. J. Ayala, *J. Heredity* 63 (1977): 3.

[11] M. Grene, *Encounter* (Nov. 1959), pp. 48-50.

Chardin proclaim that all theories, hypotheses, and systems must bow before evolution in order to be thinkable and true. One could easily search the evolutionary literature to find many other examples that reveal the religious nature of the evolutionary world view. *It can thus be stated unequivocally that evolution is as religious as creation, and conversely, that creation is as scientific as evolution.*

Creation and Evolution are the Only Valid Alternative Theories of Origins

Evolutionists often assert that creationists have constructed a false dichotomy between creation and evolution, that there are actually many theories of origins. While it is true that there are several sub-models within the general creation model, just as there are several sub-models within the general evolution model, all theories of origins can be fitted within these two general theories. Thus, Futuyma, an evolutionist as we have noted earlier, states:

> Creation and Evolution, between them, exhaust the possible explanations for the origin of living things. Organisms either appeared on the earth fully developed or they did not. If they did not, they must have developed from preexisting species by some process of modification. If they did appear in a fully developed state, they must indeed have been created by some omnipotent intelligence.[12]

No professionally trained teacher should thus hesitate to teach the scientific evidence that supports creation as an alternative to evolution. This is recognized by Alexander, who stated that:

> No teacher should be dismayed at efforts to present creation as an alternative to evolution in biology courses; indeed at this moment creation is the only alternative to evolution. Not only is this worth mentioning, but a comparison of the two alternatives can be an excellent exercise in logic and reason. Our primary goal as educators should be to teach students to think. . . . Creation and

---

[12] D. J. Futuyma, *Science on Trial*, p. 197.

evolution in some respects imply backgrounds about as different as one can imagine. In the sense that creation is an alternative to evolution for any specific question, a case against creation is a case for evolution, and *vice versa.*[13]

In a sense, both creation and evolution are based on axioms, assertions that are assumed to be true and which have predictable consequences. In his conclusion to a paper in which he gives an axiomatic interpretation of the neo-Darwinian theory of evolution, C. Leon Harris states:

First, the axiomatic nature of the neo-Darwinian theory places the debate between evolutionists and creationists in a new perspective. Evolutionists have often challenged creationists to provide experimental proof that species have been fashioned *de novo.* Creationists have often demanded that evolutionists show how chance mutations can lead to adaptability, or to explain why natural selection has favored some species but not others with special adaptations, or why natural selection allows apparently detrimental organs to persist. We may now recognize that neither challenge is fair. If the neo-Darwinian theory is axiomatic, it is not valid for creationists to demand proof of the axioms, and it is not valid for evolutionists to dismiss special creation as unproved so long as it is stated as an axiom.[14]

That belief in creation and evolution is *exactly parallel* was frankly stated by the prominent British biologist and evolutionist, L. Harrison Matthews. Matthews thus states:

. . . The fact of evolution is the backbone of biology, and biology is thus in the peculiar position of being a science founded on an unproved theory—is it then a science or a faith? Belief in the

[13] R. D. Alexander, in *Evolution versus Creationism: The Public Education Controversy* (Phoenix: Oryx Press, 1983), p 91.
[14] C. L. Harris, *Perspectives in Biology and Medicine* (Winter 1975), p. 179.

theory of evolution is thus exactly parallel to belief in special creation—both are concepts which
believers know to be true but neither, up to the
present, has been capable of proof.[15]

Teaching Both Theories of Origins is an Educational Imperative

Thus, since creation is as scientific as evolution, and evolution is as religious as creation; since creation and evolution between them exhaust the
possible explanations for origins; a comparison of the two alternatives can be
excellent exercises in logic and reason; no theory in science should be allowed to freeze into dogma, immune from the challenge of alternative theories; academic and religious freedoms are guaranteed by the United States
Constitution; public schools are supported by the taxes derived from all citi-
zens; therefore, in the public schools in the United States, the scientific evidences which support creation should be taught along with the scientific
evidences which support evolution in a philosophically neutral manner devoid of references to any religious literature.

---

[15] L. H. Matthews, Introduction to *The Origin of Species*, C. Darwin
(reprint. London: J. M. Dent and Sons, Ltd., 1971), p. x.

Chapter Two

Creation/Evolution—The Scientific Evidence

The Science of Thermodynamics

Evolutionary theories on the origin of the universe assume that a primordial explosion of a cosmic egg (the so-called "Big Bang Theory") or an event of some kind produced an early universe that essentially consisted of nothing more than hydrogen gas along with a small proportion of helium. This gas expanded into the vast reaches of the universe to the point where its density was less than the best vacuum producible by man. Out of this extremely thin and rapidly expanding gas, according to theory, stars and galaxies created themselves, our solar system created itself, and finally on planet Earth, animals and plants gradually and spontaneously created themselves. If this scenario is true, then man, with his 30 trillion cells of over 200 varieties and a brain containing 12 billion cells with 120 trillion connections, is ultimately the product of hydrogen gas, natural laws, and time, plus nothing.

Thus, hydrogen gas, and in fact all matter, must have an inherent tendency to self-organize itself, converting itself from disorder to order, from simple to complex, from primordial chaos to the cosmos. This should be a universal property of matter, so powerful and all-pervasive that it could easily be detected and recognized by scientists. We should thus have a natural law or set of natural laws which describe this tendency of matter towards self-organization, structure and complexity.

On the other hand, if creation is true, matter would not be expected to have a tendency to organize itself into higher and higher levels of

11

organization. If, however, something has happened since creation to change the original created state, this change could only be in a downward direction. Thus, based on the creation model, matter might be expected to have a natural tendency to go from order to disorder, from complex to simple.

What have scientists actually discovered out there in the real world? What is the universal tendency of matter? First we note that no scientist has ever detected a tendency of matter towards self-organization. Matter does not tend to promote itself from disorder to order, or from simple to complex. No such law is known in science. On the other hand, there is a natural tendency of matter to go in exactly the opposite direction. This tendency is so universal, so all-pervasive, so unfailing, it is called a law of science—the Second Law of Thermodynamics.

> There is a general tendency of all observed systems to go from order to disorder, reflecting dissipation of energy available for future transformation—the law of increasing entropy.[16]

> All real processes go with an increase of entropy. The entropy also measures the randomness, or lack of orderliness of the system: the greater the randomness, the greater the entropy.[17]

> Another way of stating the second law then is: "The universe is constantly getting more disorderly!" Viewed that way, we can see the second law all about us. We have to work hard to straighten a room, but left to itself it becomes a mess again very quickly and very easily. Even if we never enter it, it becomes dusty and musty. How difficult to maintain houses and machinery and our own bodies in perfect working order; how easy to let them deteriorate. In fact, all we have to do is nothing, and everything deteriorates, collapses, breaks down, wears out, all by itself—and that is what the second law is all about.[18]

---

[16] R. B. Lindsay, *American Scientist*, 56 (1968): 100.

[17] H. Blum, *American Scientist*, 43 (1955): 595.

[18] I. Asimov, *Smithsonian Institution Journal* (June 1970), p. 6.

If, as these scientists state, that is what the Second Law of Thermodynamics is all about, then indeed there is an obvious and fatal contradiction between the theory of evolution and the Second Law of Thermodynamics. The natural laws and natural processes that now govern the universe are leading inexorably to its death and destruction, and if, as evolutionists believe, these natural laws and processes are all there is and all there ever has been, how then could these same natural laws and processes have created the universe in the first place? Is it possible for the same processes that are destroying the universe to have been responsible for its origin? What sort of tortured logic must one use to reach such an impossible conclusion?

Certainly there is no doubt that the Second Law of Thermodynamics applies to an isolated system (an isolated system is a system on which no work is being performed by anything on the outside and a system into which nothing is being brought in from the outside). Everything that takes place within an isolated system occurs by a process of self-transformation. According to the Second Law, such a system will inevitably become more random, less orderly, less complex—it will never, absolutely never, become more ordered, more complex, more highly structured. Yet evolutionists believe that the universe is an isolated system which transformed itself from primordial chaos and simplicity into its present state of vast complexity, structure, and organization, clearly in contradiction to the Second Law of Thermodynamics. What an incredible faith! Creation scientists reject this pseudoscientific faith and accept the empirically established fact that the universe cannot be an isolated system that created itself—there must be a Creator external to and independent of the natural universe that was responsible for its origin.

The usual answer of evolutionists to the creationists arguments against evolution based on the Second Law is that the Second Law applies only to an isolated system but not to an open system receiving energy from the outside. Thus, they say, the earth is an open system, receiving an enormous amount of energy from the sun, far more than would be required to fuel the evolutionary process here on the earth. This is an exceedingly naive and totally inadequate answer.

First, in the evolutionary view, the universe is an isolated system, so there is no doubt that the Second Law applies to the origin of the universe. Therefore, the universe could not have created itself naturally. Secondly, suggesting that order and complexity can be generated in one portion of the universe at the expense of another portion of the universe is circular reasoning, for it leaves unanswered where did the other portion of the universe get its order and complexity which is being utilized to generate order and complexity in the first portion?

Thirdly, the simple expenditure of energy without a proper energy conversion system and an adequate control system will not generate and maintain a complex and dynamically functional system. Raw, uncontrolled energy is destructive, not constructive. Thus, Beck and Simpson (both evolutionists), in an unguarded moment, admitted that:

> ... the simple expenditure of energy is not sufficient to develop and maintain order. A bull in a China shop performs work, but he neither creates nor maintains organization. The work needed is *particular* work; it must follow specifications; it requires information on how to proceed.[19]

For example, we know that cars do not spontaneously run uphill: they spontaneously run downhill. If a car spontaneously ran uphill, it would be a clear violation of the Second Law. One can get a car to go uphill without violating the Second Law, however, but it involves more than merely expending energy. If, as evolutionists usually maintain, the simple expenditure of energy is sufficient to circumvent the Second Law of Thermodynamics, all we would have to do is pour a can of gasoline over the car and light a match. Common experience tells us, however, that the car doesn't go uphill—it goes up in smoke. To get the car to go uphill we must place the gasoline into the gas tank, from which it is fed into the motor—an energy conversion system. This motor converts the chemical energy of the gasoline into mechanical energy which, coupled with a proper drive chain, drives the car uphill.

In addition to an energy conversion system, the entire system must be under proper control. Without this control, the automobile would not run uphill, it would just run off into the ditch. Replace the human operators in an automobile factory with monkeys and not a single automobile would ever be built.

The energy from the sun can be utilized by living things here on the earth only because of the existence of green plants. Furthermore, green plants have the capability of converting radiant energy from the sun into chemical energy only because they possess photosynthesis. Photosynthesis, however, is an incredibly complex energy conversion system. Not only is this so, but

---

[19] G. G. Simpson and W. Beck, *Life—An Introduction to Biology* (New York: Harcourt, Brace and World, 1965), p. 466.

photosynthesis must be coupled with the complex, marvelously integrated metabolic machinery of the plant, and the whole must be regulated and continuously controlled. This control ultimately resides, we believe, in the genetic system of the plant, a system so complex that little about its structure and function is understood by scientists.

For order, complexity, structure and organization to be formed within a system, four conditions must first be met:

1. The system must be open to the outside

2. An adequate outside energy source must be available

3. Energy conversion systems must be available

4. The system must be under proper control

In any naturalistic evolutionary origin of the universe, *none* of these conditions are met, and on the hypothetical primordial earth only the first two conditions could be met—there were no energy conversion systems or control systems. All evolutionary scenarios for the origin of life thus employ the simple expenditure of energy, nothing more than a bull in a china shop approach. To imagine that under these conditions the complex machinery necessary for life would spontaneously create itself is contrary to all common experience available from the science of thermodynamics. In fact, if complex molecules, such as protein or DNA, were present under such circumstances, they would be rapidly destroyed by ultraviolet light and other energy sources (even simple gases such as methane and ammonia are rapidly broken down to more simple substances by ultraviolet light).

Creation scientists thus reject the scientifically untenable notion that the universe created itself following some primordial "big bang," or that life arose spontaneously on this planet. Creationists are true scientists, accepting the inevitable conclusions from the empirical facts of science. Evolutionists, on the other hand, having adopted a theory of origins before which "all theories, all hypotheses, all systems must henceforward bow and which they must satisfy in order to be thinkable and true," insist on attempting to force the data to fit the theory, and failing, they simply ignore the logical consequences.

The Origin of the Universe

We have already described above why, in view of the science of thermodynamics, the universe could not have created itself. There are many other contradictions between theories on the origin of stars, galaxies and planets and physical laws and processes. The "Big Bang" theory of the origin of the universe has some fatal weaknesses, and as a consequence has fallen on hard times within evolutionary circles. For example, according to the theory, the exploding cosmic egg supposedly produced hydrogen gas which expanded radially outward. In the real universe, however, everything is rotating—planets, stars, clusters of stars, galaxies, and clusters of galaxies. It would require massive forces to change the radial motion of that vast quantity of matter into angular motion. A cardinal principle of science is that every effect must have an adequate cause. What is the cause (or the causes) of this angular motion found everywhere in the universe? This question remains unanswered.

How does a uniform, homogeneous, rapidly expanding cloud of hydrogen gas convert itself into planets, stars, and galaxies? Why wouldn't the gas simply continue to expand forever? Cosmologists have begun to express their doubts about the Big Bang scenario. For example, Seiden has said:

> The standard Big Bang model does not give rise to lumpiness. That model assumes the universe started out as a globally smooth, homogeneous expanding gas. If you apply the laws of physics to this model, you get a universe that is uniform, a cosmic vastness of evenly distributed atoms with no organization of any kind.[20]

Sir Fred Hoyle, one of the world's foremost astronomers, has expressed outright opposition to the theory.[21,22] Concerning the Big Bang theory, Hoyle has said:

> But the interesting quark transformations are almost immediately over and done with, to be followed by a little rather simple nuclear physics, to be followed by what? By a dull-as-ditchwater expansion which degrades itself adiabatically until it

---

[20] B. Patrusky, *Science 81* (June), p. 96.
[21] F. Hoyle, *New Scientist* 92 (1981): 523.
[22] F. Hoyle, *Science Digest*, 92 (1984): 84.

is incapable of doing anything at all. The notion that galaxies form, to be followed by an active astronomical history, is an illusion. Nothing forms, the thing is as dead as a doornail.[21]

Sir Hermann Bondi, another well-known British astronomer, sums up the situation by stating:

As an erstwhile cosmologist, I speak with feeling of the fact that theories of the origin of the Universe have been disproved by present day empirical evidence, as have various theories of the origin of the Solar System.[23]

In fact, the difficulties with the theory have become so apparent that recently an attempt has been initiated to replace the Big Bang theory with what has been called the "inflationary universe" theory.[24,25] According to this theory the universe began with something the size of an electron. This cosmic "electron" then began to rapidly inflate itself, and somehow during this expansion the universe created itself. This scenario actually requires a series of miracles. These are:

1. The existence of the "electron" itself, for which no explanation is possible.

2. The initiation of the expansion—the evolutionary cosmologists humbly admit that they do not know what happened during the first 10^{-43} second of the expansion.

3. The creation of the universe essentially from nothing, or *ex nihilo* creation.

4. During its expansion, the rate of expansion of the nascent universe had to be incredibly precise or it would either have collapsed back on itself or it would have simply continued to expand forever without forming stars, planets, and galaxies. According to Michael Turner, the probability of the universe expanding at that precise speed is equal to the probability of someone throwing a dart across the universe and hitting a target

---

[23] H. Bondi, *New Scientist* 87 (1980): 611.

[24] R. Gore, *National Geographic* (June 1983), pp. 704-749.

[25] A. H. Guth and P. J. Steinhardt, *Scientific American* 250 (1984): 116-128.

on the most distant quasar one millimeter in diameter! What a miracle of miracles!

It is difficult to believe that evolutionists would suggest the above scenario as an attempt to provide a "naturalistic" theory on how the universe originated. The above seems to provide sufficient reasons to deflate the inflationary universe theory, but no doubt critics of the theory will soon provide others.

As a matter of fact evolutionary astronomers have already been forced to suggest modifications of the inflationary universe theory. During the past decade astronomers have discovered that, contrary to predictions that matter would have been evenly distributed throughout the universe by the Big Bang, the universe is exceedingly lumpy. The existence of huge superstructures and huge voids in space has been discovered.[26,27] Consequently evolutionary cosmologists have been required to suggest the existence of exotic unseen undetectable matter that was unevenly distributed at the beginning of the Big Bang, resulting in the gravitational formation of huge structures in the universe. The gravitation required would be so great that this unseen exotic matter would have to constitute 95 to 99 percent of all the matter in the universe! Since it cannot be seen, it must be dark. Since it is not giving off any detectable radiation, it must be cold. Thus, it has been called "cold dark matter." This cold dark matter is strictly imaginary. It has been invented in an attempt to save the Big Bang theory (or modified inflationary theory) from failure. Evolutionary cosmology is not an observational science. It has become a theoretical exercise based on wishful thinking. Evolutionary astronomers believe in a cosmological Santa Claus.

Even if cold dark matter exists, even if the fluctuations in the background radiation of one thirty millionth of a degree that supposedly have been detected are real, these are not sufficient to generate these huge superstructures in the universe. John Travis, commenting on the remarkable results of Nicolai da Costa, Geller, and Huchra, writes:

> The structures revealed by this celestial coverage are certainly sowing confusion. "We see these large-scale features and we don't know how to make them. We don't know how to make the structure of the universe," says Geller. For

---

[26] L. Nicolai da Costa, Margaret Geller, and John Huchra, *Astrophysical Journal (Letters)* (20 March 1994).

[27] Joseph Silk, Nature 295 (1982): 367-368.

instance, minor energy fluctuations [as suggested by purported variations in the background radiation] that cosmologists argue existed in the early universe appear to be insufficient seeds to give rise to such prodigious clusters of galaxies. "Gravity can't, over the age of the universe, amplify these irregularities enough," Geller explains.

The puzzle of large-scale structure is likely to get even tougher in the future.[28]

Even prior to these findings the theory of cold dark matter (CDM) was being challenged. Commenting on the results obtained by the Infrared Astronomy Satellite by Saunders and his co-workers,[29] David Lindley writes:

But now Saunders *et al* say that the CDM theory, like many of its predecessors, must be discarded. They argue that the picture of the galaxy distribution given by the Infrared Astronomy Satellite (IRAS) is, on the largest scales, in clear contradiction with what CDM would have. This disavowal of CDM is all the more remarkable for coming from a group of authors that includes some of the theory's long-time supporters.[30]

Thus, even a cosmological Santa Claus, providing imaginary cold dark matter, or the supposed one thirty millionth of a degree fluctuations in the background radiation, cannot save the Big Bang theory or its inflationary universe modifications. All attempts to provide a naturalistic evolutionary origin of the universe have failed.

What about the formation of stars? As one cosmologist has said, if stars didn't exist it would be easy enough to explain why they shouldn't exist. Of course, stars do exist, and evolutionists feel compelled to explain their origin, but no satisfactory theory of stellar evolution exists. There are obvious difficulties. For example, it is suggested in some scenarios that a portion of the hydrogen gas about one light year (approximately six trillion miles) in diameter begins to collapse on itself by gravitational attraction. Beginning at this extremely thin state at about 100° Kelvin (approximately—173° celcius),

---

[28] John Travis, *Science* 263 (1994): 1684.
[29] W. Saunders, et al. *Nature* 349 (1991): 32-28.
[30] David Lindley, *Nature* 349 (1991): 14.

the cloud collapses to form a star with an interior temperature of millions of degrees.

As the cloud collapses, it warms up, of course. There are now two opposing forces: the gravitational force pulling in and the gas pressure pushing out. Obviously, for the star to form, the gravitational force pulling in must exceed the gas pressure pushing out. Actually, the gas pressure pushing out would exceed the gravitational force pulling in by 50-100 times. There is thus no possibility that the cloud could collapse to form a star. To get around this difficulty it has been suggested that a nearby supernova or a rearrangement in the interstellar magnetic medium may occur to exert the necessary push to cause the cloud to collapse. Of course, this is no solution at all because such events cannot occur without stars, and so stars are required to make stars, and no answer is provided to the mystery where stars came from in the first place.

Naive and uninformed individuals in the general public and a few overeager cosmologists have come to believe that not only are viable theories on star formation available but that astronomers have actually seen stars form. Nothing could be further from the truth. For example, cosmologist C. J. Lada states,

> Yet, despite these efforts we have yet to observationally identify, with any certainty, a single object in the process of stellar birth! Moreover, we have not yet produced a viable theory of star formation, one capable of being tested and refined by critical experiment. In many ways, stellar birth is as much a mystery today as it was forty years ago.[31]

Evolutionists may object by claiming that creationists, in rejecting current theories on the origin of the universe, are merely trading on our present state of ignorance. No, it is not what we *don't* know that troubles us about these theories, it is what we *do* know. We now have a sufficient knowledge of the science of thermodynamics and of other physical laws and processes to exclude *all* naturalistic, mechanistic theories whereby the universe creates itself, and if the universe could not have created itself naturally then it had to be created supernaturally.

---

[31] C. J. Lada, "Star Formation: From OB Associations to Protostars," in *Star Forming Regions*, ed. M. Permbert and J. Jaguku, IAU Symposium 115 (1988).

The Origin of Life

Through an elegant series of experiments spanning two centuries, Spellanzani, Redi, Louis Pasteur and others disproved the notion of the spontaneous origin of life. As a result, the Law of Biogenesis, that life comes only from preexisting life, became part of the fabric of biology. With the rise of Darwinism, however, this demonstrated truth no longer became acceptable, and the notion of the spontaneous origin of life was resurrected. Although evolutionists are still light-years short of any comprehensive theory on how life may have arisen spontaneously, our students are told that the spontaneous origin of life on earth was almost inevitable. There are in fact a series of impassable barriers to a spontaneous evolutionary origin of life. A few of these are:

1. The absolute necessity for the exclusion of a significant quantity of oxygen from the hypothetical primordial atmosphere. If oxygen were present, all organic molecules would be oxidized to simple gases. The present atmosphere contains 21% oxygen, and evidence is accumulating that the earth has never had an atmosphere significantly different than it has at present. Furthermore, without oxygen there would be no ozone layer around the earth to absorb the highly energetic, deadly destructive ultraviolet light from the sun. No life can exist in the presence of this ultraviolet light, and yet evolutionists persist in believing that life arose in its presence.

2. The rates of destruction of all organic molecules, such as amino acids, sugars, purines and pyrimidines, etc., vastly exceed their rates of formation by raw, uncontrolled energy such as ultraviolet light and electrical discharges. Thus, no significant quantity of such products could ever form under plausible primitive earth conditions. The only reason Stanley Miller obtained a detectable quantity of a few amino acids in his famous experiment[32] was that he employed a trap to continuously remove the products. This prevented the reexposure of these products to the energy source that produced them. No plausible natural trap under primitive earth conditions has yet been conceived, however. Even if such a trap could exist, this in itself would be fatal to origin of life theories since

---

[32] S. L. Miller, *Science* 117 (1953): 528.

no energy would be available and all subsequent steps in the origin of life would require energy.

3. No method exists for producing in their natural state the large macromolecules, such as proteins, DNA and RNA, under plausible primitive earth conditions. There exists an impassable thermodynamic barrier to the spontaneous formation of such substances. It would be comparable to a newborn baby climbing the sheer 3,000-foot granite cliff of El Capitan in Yosemite Valley. Only living things possess the metabolic machinery necessary to overcome this thermodynamic barrier.

4. The formation of a single biologically active protein, DNA or RNA molecule requires the precise positioning of hundreds of sub-units, just as the 176 letters of this sentence had to be arranged in precise sequence. A protein of 100 amino acids is a rather small protein (the average protein contains 400 amino acids), and yet the probability of forming a single protein molecule of 100 of the 20 different amino acids arranged in precise order is approximately 10^{-130} (that is one chance out of the number one followed by 130 zeros). This probability is essentially equal to zero on a time scale of five billion years (the assumed age of the earth), and even if it did happen, only one single molecule of one single protein would be produced. The oceans of the world contain about 350 million cubic miles of water, so billions of tons each of hundreds of different protein, DNA and RNA molecules required to start life would have to be produced. This is flatly impossible.

5. The most primitive living cell imaginable would not only require hundreds of different protein molecules and hundreds of different kinds of DNA and RNA molecules but many other kinds of large and complex molecules such as carbohydrates and lipids. Furthermore, the simplest living cell known to science contains many complex elements, such as the cell membrane, ribosomes, the energy-generating system, etc. Finally, all of these must be precisely arranged so that the activities of the cell are properly coordinated in time and space. The purpose of every detail of the structure and function of the cell is evident. Thus, even the most primitive cell imaginable would be incredibly complex. Could such a complex apparatus arise by

chance, even ignoring all of the thermodynamic barriers to the formation of complex molecules and structures? The answer is a resounding NO!

A few years ago Sir Fred Hoyle and Dr. Chandra Wickramasinghe, Professor and Chairman of the Department of Applied Mathematics and Astronomy, University College, Cardiff, Wales, became interested in the problem of the origin of life. Both had been evolutionists and lifelong atheists. After making certain assumptions about the requirements for the origin of the simplest cell imaginable, they calculated the probability of the necessary protein enzymes arising by chance on this planet in five billion years. The probability turned out to be one chance out of the number one followed by 40,000 zeros![33] This is flatly zero, so they calculated the probability of life evolving anywhere in the universe, assuming that every star in the universe (about 100 billion times 100 billion) has a planet like the earth and that the universe is 20 billion years old. For all practical purposes according to their results, the probability is not insensibly different than zero. Sir Fred Hoyle said that the probability of the evolutionary origin of life is equal to the probability that a tornado sweeping through a junkyard would assemble a Boeing 747! One is free to believe that, of course, but it shouldn't be called science. Hoyle and Wickramasinghe are now saying that wherever life exists in the universe it had to be created. Wickramasinghe has stated that this evidence constitutes empirical evidence for the existence of God (they are not Biblical creationists, since neither believes the Genesis account of creation, but they believe life had to be created).

Did Sir Fred Hoyle and Professor Wickramasinghe become creationists because of their religion? Obviously not, for they were both atheists when they began their study. They became creationists *in spite* of the religious beliefs they held at that time. Most evolutionists assert that to hold a belief in creation is religion. According to this view, then when Hoyle and Wickramasinghe, in ignorance of the facts, held to an evolutionary view of the origin of life, that was proper science, but the moment the scientific evidence convinced them that life could not have arisen naturally, therefore life had to be created supernaturally, their views instantly ceased to be science and became religion!

Other scientists, such as Yockey,[34] Salisbury,[35] Coppedge,[36] and Wilder-Smith[37] have come to similar conclusions or have expressed serious

---

[33] F. Hoyle and C. Wickramasinghe, *Evolution From Space* (London: J.M. Dent and Sons, 1981).

[34] H. P. Yockey, *J. Theor. Biology* 67 (1977): 377.

23

doubts. A spontaneous evolutionary origin of life can be positively excluded on the basis of the proven principles of chemical thermodynamics and kinetics and the laws of probability. The theory of an evolutionary origin of life is Twentieth Century mythology.

The Evidence from Homology

Structures and organs in different creatures which are structurally similar, even though their function may be quite different, are said to be homologous, and the phenomenon is termed homology. These terms were coined by one of Darwin's contemporaries, Sir Richard Owen, at that time one of the most formidable opponents of Darwinism. Darwin and his fellow evolutionists have always assumed that such similarities constitute one of the best evidences for evolution. In ignorance of the actual scientific evidence, this conclusion, from an evolutionary view, seems to be quite logical. However, not only is there an equally plausible explanation based on creation, but the actual scientific evidence is contradictory to the evolutionist view that the possession of similar structures by different animals can be explained by inheritance from a common ancestor.

First, in many cases, perhaps most, the assumed common evolutionary ancestor of the creatures possessing homologous structures doesn't even possess the homologous structure or structures. In some cases creatures possess entire suites of similar major structures, none of which is possessed by the assumed common ancestor. It is thus necessary for evolutionists to postulate what is called parallel evolution, that is, the independent, parallel evolution of similar structures after the creatures had split off from the assumed common ancestor. It is difficult enough to imagine an evolutionary origin of a complex organ by chance. It is even more difficult to imagine that similar complex structures could arise by chance in different animals independently. It is asking too much, however, to have us believe that entire assortments of similar major structures could arise by chance independently in different animals. Evolutionists do not hesitate to invoke the miraculous as long as it can be concealed under the cloak of evolutionism.

---

[35] F. B. Salisbury, *Nature* 224 (1969): 342; *American Biology Teacher* 33 (1971): 335.

[36] J. F. Coppedge, *Evolution: Possible or Impossible?* (Grand Rapids, Michigan: Zondervan Publishing Co., 1973).

[37] A. E. Wilder-Smith, *The Creation of Life* (Wheaton, Illinois: Harold Shaw Publishers, 1970).

Absolutely devastating to the evolutionary interpretation of homology is the evidence from genetics. If homologous structures in different animals are due to inheritance from a common ancestor, then the genes which code for these structures in one creature should be similar to the same genes in the other creature. This must be true if the evolutionary interpretation is correct. Actually, according to Sir Gavin de Beer, the British biologist and evolutionist, such genes are *totally different from one another*. Because of this and a mass of other evidence contrary to predictions based on evolution, Sir Gavin entitled his Oxford Biology Reader on that subject, *Homology, An Unsolved Problem*.[38] On the final page of that booklet is found the following statement:

> It is now clear that the pride with which it was assumed that the inheritance of homologous structures from a common ancestor explained homology was misplaced; for such inheritance cannot be ascribed to identity of genes. The attempt to find "homologous" genes, except in closely related species, has been given up as hopeless.

Not only has the crucially important prediction related to homologous structures based on evolution been falsified, not only is there much other evidence related to homology that is contradictory to predictions based on evolution, but creation offers an eminently satisfactory explanation of homologous structures. Creation implies a master engineer employing similar solutions to similar problems. Just as an engineer, employing sound engineering principles, designs bridges that are similar in many respects, so the creator, the master engineer, would design similar structures for similar purposes. Thus, in many respects, the design of four-legged reptiles and of four-legged mammals would be similar, differing however in those features required for different life styles. Monkeys, apes, and humans each have grasping hands, keen eyesight, keen hearing, and relatively large brains, not because these characteristics were inherited from a common ancestor but because their respective life styles require these characteristics. On balance, then, the evidence from homology is strongly in favor of creation.

The Evidence from Embryology

The notion that an organism recapitulates its evolutionary history during development of the embryo became so thoroughly entrenched in

---

[38] G. de Beer, *Homology, An Unsolved Problem* (London: Oxford University Press, 1971).

evolutionary thought that it became known as the "biogenetic law." Darwin, in fact, considered that the evidence for evolution from embryology was second to none. Even though this theory is still widely taught in high school and college biology books, it has been thoroughly discredited. This led the evolutionary biologist Walter J. Bock of Columbia University to remark that ". . . the biogenetic law has become so deeply rooted in biological thought that it cannot be weeded out in spite of its having been demonstrated to be wrong by numerous subsequent scholars."[39]

It is still being claimed, for example, that the human embryo at one stage of its development has gill slits, demonstrating the fact that a fish was a distant ancestor of man. At no time in its development, however, does a human embryo ever have slits into the throat nor does a human embryo ever have gills. If a human embryo never has gills and never has slits, it is certain it never has gill slits. The human embryo has a series of pharyngeal pouches, or a series of bars and grooves, in the neck region that resemble structures in the neck region of the fish. That these resemblances are merely superficial, however, is shown by the fact that in the human embryo the so-called "gill-slits" do not develop into respiratory organs but develop into the lower jaw, structures in the middle ear, and several glands. Furthermore, recently an instrument called a fetoscope has been developed by which the development of the human embryo can be observed and photographed. This has shown that every stage in the development of the human embryo, just as predicted on the basis of creation, is uniquely human.[40] The development of the human embryo thus reveals no evidence for evolution but provides empirical support for creation.

The Evidence from Vestigial Organs

A vestigial organ has been defined as an organ found in a present-day organism that has no function but which was a useful, functional organ in an evolutionary ancestor. About a century ago, Wiederscheim listed about 180 vestigial organs for man. These included the appendix, tonsils, coccyx (the tailbone), pituitary gland, pineal gland, and the thymus gland. The results of scientific and medical research has now reduced that list practically to zero as the true function of these organs has been discovered. All of the above-mentioned organs, for example, are now known to have important functions. In an article published recently in *Evolutionary Theory*, evolutionist S.R. Scadding states his conviction that "'vestigial organs' provide no evidence

---

[39] W. J. Bock, *Science*, 164 (1969): 687.
[40] S. Schwabenthan, *Parents* (Oct. 1979), p. 50.

for evolutionary theory."[41] Again, a prediction based on evolutionary theory has been falsified and the prediction of creation scientists that the true function of these organs would eventually be discovered has been verified.

The Evidence from Molecular Biology

The amino acid sequences of many proteins have been determined. These proteins include enzymes, electron-transmitters, oxygen-carriers, and hormones. It has been found that in many cases proteins that have the same function in different animals, such as the cytochromes or the hemoglobins, have a very similar amino acid sequence in different organisms. Those proteins, such as the cytochromes, which have a similar amino acid sequence are said to be homologous. Furthermore, it has been generally determined that those homologous proteins found in creatures which closely resemble each other differ less from one another than those homologous proteins found in creatures that do not closely resemble one another. Thus, the cytochrome C found in man is more similar to those found in the apes than it is to that found in a rat or a snake. Evolutionists have eagerly seized upon this evidence as "proof"of evolution.

We must first point out that this sort of evidence is of no help whatsoever in weighing the credibility of creation versus the credibility of evolution. This similarity in the biochemistry of all living things *must* be true, regardless of the explanation for their origins. Let us suppose, for example, that plants, animals, and humans were each created with a different type of amino acids, sugars, purines, pyrimidines, etc. What would we eat? We could eat neither plants nor animals since we could not utilize the amino acids, sugars, and other substances found in these organisms. The only thing we could eat would be each other! That would obviously be an impossible solution. Thus, animals, plants and humans had to have the same amino acids, sugars, purines, pyrimidines, etc. This fact would then determine that the biochemistry of all plants, animals and man had to be similar, since the biochemical machinery of each had to be designed to metabolize the same substances. This fact was recognized by (then evolutionist) Kenyon and evolutionist Steinman when they stated that:

> It could be argued that the universality of much
> of biochemistry is merely consistent with the con-
> cept of a common ancestral population but does

---

[41] S. R. Scadding, *Evolutionary Theory*, 5 (1981): 173.

not in any sense prove it since the same basic re-
action patterns may be *required* for life.[42]

Furthermore, since our external morphology is at least to some extent
shaped by our internal chemistry, we would expect that creatures that more
closely resemble one another would have biochemistries that are more similar than those in creatures that do not closely resemble one another. Thus, the
predictions concerning molecular homology based on creation and evolution
would be substantially the same.

The evidence from molecular biology has, however, produced some
serious difficulties for evolutionary theory, and as more and more data on
molecular structures have become known, the more serious the difficulties
have become. According to evolutionary theory, evolution is a mechanistic
process which should produce data that is consistent with a mechanistic theory. If data appear that are inconsistent or contradictory to those predicted by
the theory, the theory is weakened. If a sufficient body of such contradictory
evidence accumulates, then the theory is seriously jeopardized. That situation
is being approached with evolutionary theory relative to predictions concerning molecular biology as more and more predictions concerning evolution
and molecular structures are being falsified. Space permits us to describe
only a few.

The insulins of the sperm whale and of the fin whale are identical to
those of the dog and the pig but differ from that of the sei whale.[43]

There are 18 differences when the amino acid sequence of guinea pig
insulin is compared to either human insulin or to the insulin from a fellow ro-
dent, the rat[44] The structure of cytochrome C of the rattlesnake varies in 22
places compared to the cytochrome C of the turtle, another reptile, but only
in 14 places when compared to human insulin.[45] When the cytochromes C of
two supposedly closely related organisms, *Desulfovibrio desulfuricans* and
Desulfovibrio vulgaris, are compared, it is found that they differ markedly in
amino acid composition.[46] The amino acid sequence of lysozyme of Emden

---

[42] D. H. Kenyon and G. Steinman, *Biochemical Predestination* (New
York: McGraw-Hill Book Co., 1969), p. 5.

[43] R. V. Eck and M. O. Dayhoff, *Atlas of Protein Sequence and
Structure* (Silver Springs, Maryland: National Biomedical Research
Foundation, 1966), p. 110.

[44] *Ibid.*, p. 191.

[45] *Ibid.*, p. 170.

[46] H. Drucker et al., *Biochemistry* 9 (1970): 1515.

goose egg-white is not homologous at all (or doubtfully very weakly so) with lysozyme of hen egg-white.[47]

According to evolutionary theory, mammals are more closely related to reptiles than to amphibians. However, mammalian luteinizing hormone releasing hormone is identical to that of amphibians but differs from that of reptiles.[48]

Based on his research findings, evolutionist Dr. Christian Schwabe is suggesting a drastic revision of evolutionary theory. From the results of his molecular studies of hormones, Schwabe contends that the theory that all life forms are related through common ancestry does not appear to be true.[49] Schwabe contends that these data supports the fact that each basic type had a separate origin (this theory is called polyphyletic evolution). Schwabe is thus saying exactly what creationists have been saying all along—that all creatures have *not* shared a common ancestry but that there was a multitude of separate and distinct origins. Schwabe and creation scientists differ, of course, as to how each separate type originated in the first place. Nevertheless, if Schwabe and the creation scientists are correct in their contention that the data of molecular biology supports multiple origins rather than descent from a common ancestor, then evolutionists are deprived of what they consider to be one of their strongest arguments for evolution. It is of great significance that the data are now sufficiently strong to swing an evolutionist of Dr. Schwabe's very considerable knowledge and research experience over to the views of creation scientists against a common ancestry of organisms.

Michael Denton holds an M.D. degree and a Ph.D. in molecular biology from British universities. He is neither a Christian nor a professing creationist, but his book, *Evolution: A Theory in Crisis*, is a devastating critique of evolutionary theory. On every count, according to Denton, evolution strikes out. According to Denton, molecular biology, rather than supporting evolution, provides evidence directly contradictory to the evidence predicted. Denton points out that protein sequence data reveals the same large systematic gaps between basically different kinds that are also evident from the

---

[47] M. G. Grutter, L. H. Weaver and B. W. Matthews, *Nature* 303 (1983): 828.

[48] J. A. King, *Science* 206 (1979): 67.

[49] Christian Schwabe and G. W. Warr, *Perspectives in Biology and Medicine*, 27(3, Spring 1984): 465-484; C. Swabe, *Trends in Biochemical Sciences* 11(July 1986): 280-283; C. Swabe, *Comp. Biochem. Physiol.* 1078 (1994): 167-177.

fossil record. With reference to the so-called evolutionary molecular clock based on protein sequence data, Denton states:

> Despite the fact that no convincing explanation of how random evolutionary processes could have resulted in such an ordered pattern of diversity, the idea of uniform rates of evolution is presented in the literature as if it were an empirical discovery. The hold of the evolutionary paradigm is so powerful, that an idea which is more like a principle of medieval astrology than a serious twentieth-century scientific theory has become a reality for evolutionary biologists.[50]

Many other investigators have pointed out the essential futility of attempts to use data from protein sequences, DNA and RNA to establish evolutionary relationships. For example (and there are many) Weishampel, Dodson, and Osmolska state:

> Molecular data on tetrapod phylogeny are equivocal regarding the relationships of birds and crocodilians. Some analyses do pair these two groups, but many tend to link birds and mammals more closely. However, other protein sequence analyses give every other imaginable pairing of tetrapod groups and their significance is debatable.[51]

In spite of all the claims that have been made by evolutionists for the utility of protein sequence analyses in establishing evolutionary relationships, it is obvious that if such data can be so interpreted by various scientists to establish every imaginable pairing of such important groups as tetrapods (amphibians, reptiles, mammals, and birds), such data are useless and those claims are false. The data actually are much more in accord with predictions based on creation than evolution.

---

[50] Michael Denton, *Evolution: A Theory in Crisis* (London: Burnett Books, 1985), p. 306. Available from Woodbine and Associates, 6510 Bells Mill Road, Bethesda, MD 20817.

[51] D.B. Weishampel, Peter Dodson, and Halszka Osmolska, eds. *The Dinosauria* (Berkeley: University of Chicago Press, 1990), p. 12.

Chapter Three

The Evidence From the Fossil Record

According to the generally accepted notion about evolution, all living forms on the earth today, both plants and animals, have descended with modification from a single form of life which itself had arisen from a dead, inanimate world. This diversification, it is said, has occurred during the past three billion years or so, and has produced the more than two million species that now exist and millions more that have become extinct. Billions times billions times billions of these creatures would have lived and died during that vast stretch of time.

The so-called neo-Darwinian evolutionists believe that practically all of evolution has occurred very slowly and gradually by a combination of micromutations and natural selection. More recently, more and more evolutionists have finally begun to recognize the fact that there is little or no evidence for gradual change in the fossil record. They are suggesting a more jerky type of evolution whereby species exist for millions of years with essentially no change and then for some unknown reason by some unknown mechanism rapidly give rise to new species. This notion is called punctuated equilibria. A few have become so discouraged by the absence of transitional forms they have even suggested what has been called the "hopeful monster" mechanism. Those who advocate this theory say that transitional forms are not found because none ever existed. Thus, for example, the first bird hatched from a reptilian egg! What they suggest, in other words, is that by some means, a change took place in the embryonic stage of development (this is called a systemic mutation or a macromutation) that causes a drastic restructuring of the organism. No one has ever seen anything like this happen, of course, and this notion only illustrates the desperate position in which some evolutionists feel placed by the absence of transitional forms.

Predictions Based on Evolution

By either the neo-Darwinian or the punctuated equilibria mechanism of evolution, a vast number of intermediate stages would have been produced as millions of species evolved during many hundreds of millions of years. If these ideas are correct, the number of transitional forms that would have existed in the past would be enormous. Our museums now contain in excess of 250,000 different fossil species represented by tens of millions of catalogued fossils (the Smithsonian Natural History Museum contains 40 million fossils). The fossil record has become almost immeasurably rich. Ever since Darwin, evolutionists have searched intensely for the transitional forms that are predicted on the basis of evolutionary theory. If the theory is true, these museums should contain tens of thousands of undoubted transitional forms, showing, for example, the intermediate stages between single-celled organisms and the complex invertebrates, transitional forms between invertebrates and fishes, transitional forms between fish and amphibia, between reptiles and birds and mammals, between apes and people, etc. There should be no doubt about the fact of evolution, no question, no dispute, no debate. Transitional forms should be as common, and actually much more so, than terminal forms.

Predictions Based on Creation

On the other hand, if creation is true, each separately created type of plants and animals (each such type would have a particular unique morphological design and would include all organisms which have shared a unique and exclusive common genetic origin) would appear in the fossil record fully formed at its first appearance and would be separated by a distinct gap from all other created types. The gaps between all basic created types would be systematic. For example, there are 32 orders of mammals. These include, to name a few, the flying mammals or bats; marine mammals, such as whales and dolphins; the rodents; the hoofed animals; the carnivores; and the primates, including prosimians, monkeys, apes, and man. The creation scientist would predict that no transitional forms or intermediate links would be found between any of these 32 orders of mammals and any of the various types of reptiles. Furthermore, within each mammalian order, each basic type would stand isolated from all others with no intermediate links. Thus, within the

32

order Primates, prosimians, monkeys, apes, and man would be separate and distinct with no transitional forms linking these distinctly different types. Finally, separate and distinct created types within each of these basic categories can be distinguished. Among the apes, for example, gibbons, orangutans, chimpanzees and gorillas would each constitute a separate created type. Man, on the other hand, stands alone, there being a single species, *Homo sapiens* within the family of man, the Hominidae. Creation scientists would predict that no transitional forms will be found linking these distinctly separate created forms.

Thus, the predictions concerning the fossil record based on creation and evolution contrast sharply with one another:

Evolution: Gradual change of "lower" forms into "higher" forms, with vast numbers of transitional forms or intermediate types.

Creation: The abrupt appearance, fully formed, of each created type and the total absence of organisms that could be interpreted as constituting transitional forms between these basic types.

The Fossil Record Provides Powerful Support for Creation

Ever since Darwin, the fossil record has been an embarrassment to evolutionists. Darwin knew that the fossil record did not provide the evidence demanded by his theory, but felt confident that future work in paleontology would produce the required transitional forms that were missing. We are now 136 years after Darwin and the situation is actually worse for evolutionary theory than it was then. An intense search for the hoped for transitional forms has only served to solidify the gaps.

In 1977 Stephen Jay Gould, one of the leading spokesmen for evolution theory today, confessed that "The extreme rarity of transitional forms in the fossil record persists as the trade secret of paleontology."[52] Unfortunately for evolutionary apologists, that fact is rapidly losing its status as a trade secret and has found its way into the popular press. Thus, in an article significantly entitled "Is Man a Subtle Accident?" which appeared in *Newsweek* (November 3, 1980), we read that:

> The missing link between man and the apes, whose absence has comforted religious fundamentalists since the days of Darwin, is merely the most glamorous of a whole hierarchy of phantom

---

[52] S. J. Gould, *Natural History* 86 (1977): 14.

creatures. . . .The more scientists have searched
for the transitional forms that lie between species,
the more they have been frustrated.

An article by Francis Hitching which appeared in the April 1982 issue of *Life Magazine* was entitled "Was Darwin Wrong?" Hitching's doubt about Darwin's theory was primarily based on the failure to find the transitional forms required by the Darwinian mechanism for evolution. In 1982 the British Broadcasting Corporation produced a TV program entitled "Did Darwin Get It Wrong?" The rationale for the program and the inspiration for the title was again the failure to find the transitional forms demanded by Darwin's theory.

Ever since Darwin, creation scientists have called attention to the fact that the fossil record is remarkably in accord with creation while failing to produce what is expected by evolutionists. While most evolutionists still cling to their faith in evolution, in latter times more and more are admitting that there is little, if any, evidence for gradual change in the fossil record. Corner, a Cambridge University botanist and evolutionist states that:

> Much evidence can be adduced in favor of the theory of evolution—from biology, biogeography and paleontology, but I still think that, to the unprejudiced, the fossil record of plants is in favor of special creation.[53]

This is so because each major type of plant appears in the fossil record fully-formed from the start, with no transitional forms to suggests its origin from some "lower" form.

Kitts, a paleontologist and evolutionist at the University of Oklahoma, has remarked that:

> Despite the bright promise that paleontology provides a means of "seeing" evolution, it has presented some nasty difficulties for evolutionists, the most notorious of which is the presences of "gaps" in the fossil record. Evolution requires intermediate forms between species and paleontology does not provide them.[54]

[53] E. J. H. Corner, in *Contemporary Botanical Thought*, ed. A. M. MacLeod and L. S. Cobley (Chicago: Quadrangle Books, 1961), p. 97.
[54] D. B. Kitts, *Evolution* 28 (1974): 467.

Concerning the hypothetical evolutionary phylogenetic tree, Colin Patterson, senior paleontologist at the British Museum of Natural History, states that:

> We have access to the tips of the tree; the tree itself is theory, and people who pretend to know about the tree and to describe what went on it—how the branches came off and the twigs came off—are, I think, telling stories."[55]

In a speech he gave at the American Museum of Natural History,[56] Patterson admitted that he had duped himself into believing that he understood evolution but now he realized there was not one thing he knew about it. It was clear to him now, he said, that in accepting evolution he had moved from science into *faith*. He cited several examples in which predictions based on the theory had been precisely falsified.

Sir Edmund Leach has recently added his voice to the growing chorus of evolutionists who are candidly admitting the true nature of the fossil record. He states: "Missing links in the sequence of fossil evidence were a worry to Darwin. He felt sure they would eventually turn up, but they are still missing and seem likely to remain so."[57]

In Woodruff's review of a book on evolution he says that ". . . fossil species remain unchanged throughout most of their history and the record fails to contain a single example of a significant transition."[58] If evolution were true, the fossil record should document *many thousands* of significant transitions but the record fails to produce a *single example*.

The British evolutionist, Mark Ridley, apparently recognized that the fossil record offers little, if any, support for evolution, for he advises that ". . . no real evolutionist, whether gradualist or punctuationist, uses the fossil record as evidence in favor of the theory of evolution as opposed to special creation."[59] If evolution is true, how can this be? If evolution has actually occurred, what better evidence for evolution could one expect than the historical record inscribed in the rocks? In contrast to Ridley's aversion to the use

---

[55] Brian Leith, *The Listener,* 106 (1981): 390.

[56] Transcript from tape, recorded November 5, 1981 at the American Museum of Natural History.

[57] E. R. Leach, *Nature* 293 (1981): 19.

[58] D. S. Woodruff, *Science* 208 (1980): 716.

[59] Mark Ridley, *New Scientist* 90 (1981): 830.

of the fossil record for the support of evolution, creation scientists do not hesitate to employ the fossil record in support of creation, declaring that this record provides powerful *positive* evidence for creation. In the following sections are documented only a few of the vast multitude of gaps in the fossil record.

The Monumental Gap Between Single-Celled Organisms and Complex, Multicellular Invertebrates

Evolutionists believe that rocks of the so-called Cambrian Period were formed from sediments that were slowly deposited during a time period from 520 million years B.P. (before the present) to about 500 million years B.P. In these rocks fossils of a vast array of complex invertebrates are found. These include, for example, fossils of such diverse types as sponges, jellyfish, clams, snails, worms, trilobites, brachiopods, sea urchins, sea cucumbers, sea lillies, etc. These creatures in each case apparently appeared fully formed without a trace of any transitional forms linking them to an ancestor. Right from the start, a jellyfish was a full-fledged jellyfish, a sponge was a sponge, a trilobite was a trilobite and a sea urchin was a fully-formed sea urchin.

Douglas Futuyma is an evolutionary biologist who is a militant anti-creationist. In his book on evolutionary biology he is nevertheless forced to confess that:

> It is considered likely that all the animal phyla became distinct before or during the Cambrian, for they all appear fully formed, without intermediates connecting one phylum to another. Thus our understanding of the phylogenetic relationships among the phyla, which are a matter of some dispute, is based on inferences from their anatomy and embryology.[60]

Because of the total absence of ancestors and transitional forms evolutionists are forced to base their ideas on the origin of this vast array of complex invertebrates on the anatomy and embryology of living representatives of these invertebrates. This confession of the failure to find any evidence for the evolutionary origin is repeated over and over again in the evolutionary literature. For example, Jeffrey Levinton states:

---

[60] D. Futuyma, *Evolutionary Biology*, 2nd ed. (Sunderland, Mass.: Sinauer Associates, Inc., 1986), p. 325.

> All known animal phyla that readily fossilize
> appeared during the 60-million-year Cambrian pe-
> riod . . . the phyla do seem to have appeared sud-
> denly and simultaneously . . . All in all the facts
> still point to an explosion of complex life near the
> beginning of the Cambrian. . . . The Cambrian ex-
> plosion thus remains a mystery.[61] [Evolutionists
> are now estimating the Cambrian Period to be no
> more than 5–10 million years in duration].

Generally underlying the Cambrian rocks are the rocks of the so-called Precambrian Period. Evolutionists assume that these rocks formed during hundreds of millions of years preceding the Cambrian. Many of the rocks are undisturbed, often identical with the overlying Cambrian rocks and perfectly suitable for the preservation of fossils. In these rocks, if evolution were true, we should find the evolutionary predecessors of the Cambrian animals. Nowhere on the face of the earth, however, have we found an ancestor for a single one of the complex invertebrates found in Cambrian rocks. In the scientific literature there are now many reports of the discovery in Precambrian rocks of fossils of single-celled, soft-bodied, microscopic bacteria and algae. Evolutionists believe that these fossils are as much as three billion years old. Surely if we can find fossils of organisms like that there would be no problem in finding fossils of the vast multitude of intermediate stages that existed between these single-celled microscopic creatures and the diverse array of complex invertebrates of the Cambrian rocks. Billions times billions times billions of such intermediates would have lived and died, yet not a single fossil of an intermediate has ever been found.

In rocks allegedly about 70 million years older than the earliest Cambrian rocks are found fossils of the so-called Ediacaran Fauna. These are complex, soft-bodied invertebrates, earlier identified as jellyfish, worms, and coelenterates. Recent work has shown, however, that these creatures are very unlike creatures found in the Cambrian rocks and therefore could not possibly have been predecessors to any of the Cambrian animals.[61,62] They were in any case not intermediate in type at all, but were complex, multicellular creatures. The monumental gap between single-celled microscopic organisms and the complex Cambrian animals remains. To evolutionists this is the "major mystery in the history of life" but the creation scientist says, what greater evidence for creation could the rocks give than this sudden, explosive

---

[61] J. S. Levinton, *Scientific American* 267 (1992): 86-91.
[62] S.J. Gould, *Natural History* 93 (1984): 14.

appearance of a vast array of extremely diverse creatures without a trace of an ancestor? This is powerful positive evidence for creation.

No Transitional Forms Between Invertebrates and Fishes

Evolutionists believe that the fishes evolved from invertebrates. Fishes are, of course, members of the vertebrate sub-phylum, creatures with internal skeletons. This transition is believed to have required up to 100 million years. Surely, if evolution were true, our museums would contain tens of thousands of fossilized intermediates, documenting this remarkable transition. Not one single such fossil has ever been found! Concerning the three major types of bony fishes, for example, Todd admits that we have never found a trace of any earlier intermediate forms.[63]

White states that every major kind of fish that he knew anything about had its origin firmly based in *nothing*.[64] Arthur Strahler has published a comprehensive anti-creationist book.[65] It is instructive and most informative to read what he says about this author's claims concerning the total absence of ancestors or transitional forms for every one of the major fish classes. On page 408 Strahler says:

> Duane Gish finds from reading Alfred S. Romer's 1996 treatise, *Vertebrate Paleontology*, that mainstream paleontologists have found no fossil record of transitional chordates leading up to the appearance of the first class of fishes, the Agnatha, or of transitional forms between the primitive, jawless agnaths and the jaw-bearing class Placodermi, or of transition from the placoderms (which were poorly structured for swimming) to the class Chondrichthyes, or from those cartilaginous-skeleton sharklike fishes to the class Osteichthyes, or bony fishes (1978a, pp. 66–70; 1985, pp. 65–69). The evolution of these classes is shown in Figure 43.1. Neither says Gish, is there any record of transitional forms leading to the rise of the lungfishes and the crossopterygians from

---

[63] G. T. Todd, *American Zoology* 20(4, 1980): 757.

[64] Errol White, *Proc Linn Soc London*, 177 (1966): 8.

[65] A. N. Strahler, *Science and Earth History—The Evolution/Creation Controversy* (Buffalo: Prometheus Books, 1987).

the lobe-finned bony fishes, an evolutionary step that is supposed to have led to the rise of amphibians and ultimately to the conquest of the land by air-breathing vertebrates.

In a series of quotations from Romer (1966), Gish finds all the confessions he needs from the evolutionists that each of these classes appears suddenly and with no trace of ancestors. The absence of the transitional fossils in the gaps between each group of fishes and its ancestor is repeated in standard treatises on vertebrate evolution. Even Chris McGowan's 1984 anticreationist work, purporting to show "why the creationists are wrong," makes no mention of Gish's four pages of text on the origin of the fish classes. Knowing that McGowan is an authority on vertebrate paleontology, keen on faulting the creationists at every opportunity, I must assume that I haven't missed anything important in this area. This is one count in the creationists' charge that can only evoke in unison from the paleontologists a plea of *nolo contendere*.

It is obvious that Strahler believes in evolution not *because* of the evidence but *in spite* of the evidence. In the rocks of the earth are entombed billions times billions of fossils of complex invertebrates and untold billions of fossil fishes. If evolution is true the rocks should contain billions times billions of fossils of intermediates between the ancestral invertebrate and the fishes. It is physically impossible for such a tremendous evolutionary transition to take place during millions of years without leaving a trace. Our museum should be overflowing with the transitional forms that would reveal which invertebrate evolved into fishes and that would trace the course of that evolution. Not a single such intermediate has been found. *The issue is settled. Evolution has not taken place on this planet*. The sudden appearance, fully-formed, of all major fish types is incompatible with evolutionary theory but is *positive* evidence for creation, precisely what would be expected by creation scientists.

Systematic Gaps Between All Higher Categories of Vertebrates

George Gaylord Simpson, one of the world's leading evolutionists, has stated that: "Gaps among known orders, classes, and phyla are systematic and almost always large."[66] Evolution, however, demands an unbroken continuum, from the first emergent life form to man, but the fossil record, instead of providing even a semblance of such a continuum, is a record systematically split by gaps, with each type of distinct morphological design appearing fully formed.

According to evolution theory, fishes gave rise to amphibians. The oldest known amphibian, *Ichthyostega*, already had the basic amphibian limbs, feet and legs.[67] Its supposed fish ancestor, a rhipidistian crossopterygian, was a 100% fish with a set of fins designed for balancing, steering and locomotion in the water.[68] Its pelvic bones were small and loosely embedded in muscle, with no attachment to the vertebral column. None were needed. The fins did not and could not have supported the weight of the body. On the other hand, the pelvic bones of *Ichthyostega* were very large and firmly attached to the vertebral column, precisely the type of anatomy required for its mode of locomotion. No intermediates between ichthyostegid amphibians and their supposed crossopterygian fish ancestors have ever been found.

The origin of flight should provide an ideal test case of evolution versus creation. According to evolutionary theory, flight has arisen at least four times independently: in the flying insects; in birds; in the flying mammals, or bats; and in the flying reptiles, now extinct. Each of these transitions, from the supposed non-flying ancestor to the first flying creature, is believed to have required many millions of years. If evolution were true, museums should be overflowing with fossils documenting these transitions.

What does the record show? Not a trace of an intermediate has ever been found between the non-flying insects and flying insects,[69] although we have many fossils of each, some in remarkable states of preservation. Some of the flying reptiles had wingspreads up to 52 feet long (longer than an F-4 Phantom jet!). All of the flying reptiles appear in the fossil record fully-

---

[66] G. G. Simpson, in *Evolution of Life*, ed. Sol Tax (University of Chicago Press, 1960), p. 149.

[67] A. S. Romer, *Vertebrate Paleontology*, 3rd ed. (Chicago: University of Chicago Press, 1966), p. 88.

[68] *Ibid*, p. 68.

[69] E. C. Olson, *The Evolution of Life* (New York: The New American Library, 1965), p. 180.

formed. Not a trace of an intermediate has ever been found.[70] The oldest known fossil bat, allegedly 50 million years old, was a 100% bat, essentially identical to a modern bat.[71] Not only did it appear fully-formed with no hint of a transition from a supposed non-flying mammal, but it has undergone essentially no change in the supposed 50 million years since its first appearance. Perhaps evolutionists would claim that we can find no evidence for the origin of bats because its evolution was too fast and we see no evidence of change since its origin because evolution has been too slow!

Archaeopteryx is supposedly the world's oldest known bird. It was indeed a bird, possessing wings, perching feet, a bird-like skull, a powerful furcula (wishbone), and feathers that were identical to those of modern flying birds. No transitional forms between this bird and a reptile or between this bird and any other bird has ever been found—it stands in remarkable isolation. It does have teeth, claws on the wings, a long tail, and some other features that evolutionists allege link it to a reptilian ancestor of some kind (dinosaurs, crocodiles and thecodont reptiles each have their advocates as ancestors).

Do these characteristics indicate a reptilian ancestry for *Archaeopteryx*? Perhaps—but then perhaps not. The touraco of Africa, the hoatzin of South America, and the ostrich all have claws on the wings, but no one would suggest that any of these birds are intermediates. What about the teeth? It is true that birds surviving today do not have teeth, but it is also true that in the fossil record, just as is true with all other classes of vertebrates, some birds had teeth and some did not. Not a single intermediate has ever been found between toothed birds and toothless birds.

Many have claimed that *Archaeopteryx* could not fly, but Olson and Feduccia have documented that there was nothing in its anatomy that would have prevented it being a powered flier.[72] Some, such as John Ostrom, have argued that *Archaeopteryx* was derived from certain theropod dinosaurs, but recent studies are invalidating these claims.[73,74] Concerning *Archaeopteryx*, Gould and Eldredge have made the following interesting comments:

---

[70] *Ibid.*, p. 181.
[71] *Ibid.*, p. 182. See also G. L. Jepson, *Science* 154 (1966): 1333.
[72] S. L. Olson and A. Feduccia, *Nature* 278 (1979): 247.
[73] L. D. Martin, J. D. Stewart and K. N. Whetstone, *The Auk* 97. (1980): 86.
[74] M. J. Benton, *Nature* 305 (1983): 99.

At the higher level of evolutionary transition between basic morphological designs, gradualism has always been in trouble, though it remains the "official" position of most Western evolutionists. Smooth intermediates between Bauplane are almost impossible to construct, even in thought experiments; there is certainly no evidence for them in the fossil record (curious mosaics like *Archaeopteryx* do not count).[75]

Gould and Eldredge thus say that *Archaeopteryx* cannot be cited as an intermediate between basic morphological designs—it is merely a strange mosaic. The duck-billed platypus is another strange mosaic—no evolutionist has the faintest idea where to place that creature in any evolutionary scheme.

Swinton, an evolutionist who certainly believes that birds have evolved, and probably from reptiles, has nevertheless admitted that:

The origin of birds is largely a matter of deduction. There is no fossil evidence of the stages through which the remarkable change from reptile to bird was achieved.[76]

Recently, James Jensen has found what he believes to be the fossilized remains of a fully modern-type bird in rocks which evolutionists believe were of the same time period in which *Archaeopteryx* has been found (the rocks of the Upper Jurassic).[77]

The most damaging blows to the claims that *Archaeopteryx* represents an intermediate form between reptiles and birds comes from the discovery of Sankar Chatterjee and his colleagues at Texas Tech University of the fossils of a bird in the Dockum Formation of Texas.[78,79,80] According to Dr. Chatterjee his bird, which he named *Protoavis*, is more birdlike than *Archaeopteryx*. However, the assumed age of the Dockum Formation is 225 million years, but *Archaeopteryx* supposedly dates from only 150 million years. If

[75] S. J. Gould and Niles Eldredge, *Paleobiology* 3 (1977): 147.

[76] W. E. Swinton in *Biology and Comparative Physiology of Birds*, Vol. 1, ed. A. J. Marshall (New York: Academic Press, 1960), p. 1.

[77] J. L. Marx, *Science* 199 (1978): 284.

[78] Tim Beardsley, *Nature* 322 (1986): 677.

[79] Richard Monastersky, *Science News*, 140 (1991): 104-105.

[80] S. Chatterjee, *Phil. Trans. R. Soc. Lond. B* 332 (1991): 277-342.

Archaeopteryx is truly an intermediate between reptiles and birds, if *Protoavis* is actually 225 million years old (supposedly as old as the oldest dinosaur), and birds actually did evolve from reptiles, then *Protoavis* should be so reptilian it would hardly be recognized as on its way to becoming a bird. According to Chatterjee, however, in important aspects, it is even more bird-like than *Archaeopteryx*. This is precisely the opposite that would be predicted if birds had evolved from reptiles.

Archaeopteryx thus remains in marvelous isolation—in some ways, as in possession of teeth and claws, a strange mosaic perhaps, but a bird from its first appearance and not a link between birds and reptiles at all. We see, then, that the test case of creation versus evolution from the origin of flight produces absolutely no evidence for evolution in the case of flying insects, flying reptiles and bats. In the case of birds, instead of the series of intermediate forms that millions of years of evolution should have produced, we have one highly disputable suggested candidate—*Archaeopteryx*—"a strange mosaic that doesn't count." On a scale of one to ten, the score for creation versus evolution based on the origin of flight would be at least 9.5 in favor of creation. Again, this constitutes powerful positive evidence for creation.

Next to *Archaeopteryx* the other most frequently suggested possibility as candidates for transitional forms are the so-called mammal-like reptiles as predecessors of mammals. It is very significant that every reptile, fossil or living, has multiple bones in the jaw and a single bone in the ear, while every mammal, fossil or living, has a single jawbone (the dentary) and three bones in the ear. There are no intermediates. Supposedly during some as yet undiscovered transition, two bones of the reptilian jaw were somehow refashioned into the incus and malleus of the mammalian ear. No one has as yet, however, explained how a series of genetic mistakes could so marvelously redesign these bones so as to be perfectly engineered, nor has anyone yet explained how the creature managed to chew and to hear while dragging two bones from the jaw up into the ear. Furthermore, the essential organ of hearing in the mammal is an amazingly complex structure called the organ of Corti. This organ is not found in any reptile, nor is there any structure in the reptile from which it could have been derived. It would have had to have been created *de novo*—isn't that a bit too much to expect form a series of genetic mistakes?

When the fossil record of the mammal-like reptiles (all are included within the Synapsida, which is a subclass within the Class Reptilia) is examined we find the same systematic gaps that are found throughout the fossil record. Kemp, who has written a comprehensive review of the mammal-like reptiles, says in that review:

> Of course there are many gaps in the synapsid fossil record, with intermediate forms between the various known groups almost invariably unknown (p.3). . . . The apparent rate of morphological change in the main lineages of the mammal-like reptiles varies. The sudden appearance of new higher taxa, families and even orders, immediately after a mass extinction, with all the features more or less developed, implies a very rapid evolution (p. 327). . . . Gaps at a lower taxonomic level, species and genera, are practically universal in the fossil record of the mammal-like reptiles. In no single adequately documented case is it possible to trace a transition, species by species, from one genus to another (p. 319).[81]

If evolution is true, why are the intermediate forms, demanded by evolution, almost "invariably" unknown? There should be multitudes of transitional forms if mammals gradually evolved from reptiles supposedly during a period of about a hundred million years.

Tom Bethell, who holds a degree in the philosophy of science from Oxford University, made the following comment on the sad state of evolutionary theory:

> The great problem with the theory of evolution is that it is supported by very little evidence. A decade ago, Colin Patterson of the British Museum of Natural History said he knew of none at all. More recently, the chairman of the department of ichthyology at the American Museum of Natural History in New York said that "evidence, or proof of origins . . . of all the major groups of life, of all the minor groups of life, indeed of all the species—is weak or nonexistent when measured on an absolute scale." We are of course endlessly

---

[81] T. S. Kemp, *Mammal-Like Reptiles and the Origin of Mammals* (New York: Academic Press, 1982).

bombarded with Just-So stories, such as the recent one about mammal-like creatures walking into the sea and turning into whales, but the speculative nature of these stories is usually concealed. The story of human origins finds its way into the headlines every six months or so, the better to rub in our alleged descent from apes. But in all these primate scenarios a mountain of speculation hangs from a scrap of bone, and with every new press conference the dating of relevant events is changed by a million years or so.[82]

The Origin of Man

Nothing excites our interest in origins more than that which offers some hint concerning our own origin. More than one obscure paleoanthropologist has become famous overnight by means of sensational and extravagant claims concerning some fragmentary remains he has found which he claims are importantly related to human origins, especially if the find was made in some distant spot in Africa or Asia. In this small booklet we have space to discuss only briefly the evidence related to human origins, but a careful, thorough and objective review of that evidence shows that monkeys, apes and humans have always been separate and distinct, contrary to the notions widely disseminated in textbooks, magazines, and newspapers and on radio and television. For several decades now the australopithecines have been central figures in human evolutionary schemes. These have included the earliest find in 1924 by Raymond Dart in South Africa (*Australopithecus africanus*), a later find in 1959 in Tanzania by Louis and Mary Leakey (*Australopithecus robustus*), and recent finds in the seventies in Ethiopia by Donald Johanson (*Australopithecus afarensis*).[83] Johanson found the remains of more than a half-dozen creatures, one of which was of a female about 40% complete. He gave this female creature the name "Lucy" and has declared that "Lucy" and the associated creatures, although ape from the neck up, walked upright exactly in the manner of modern man. Johanson claimed an age of about 3.8 million years for these creatures. Johanson thus claimed that he had the oldest link between man and the apes. Because of the sensational nature of these claims which were widely disseminated by press, radio and

---

[82] Tom Bethell, *The American Spectator* (July 1994), p. 16.

[83] Donald Johanson and M. A. Edey, *Lucy, The Beginnings of Mankind* (New York: Simon and Schuster, 1981).

television, Johanson became world-famous almost overnight and now has his own Institute of Human Origins on the campus of Arizona State University in Tucson.

Since it is admitted that *A. afarensis* was essentially ape from the neck up (it was reported that when a skull was reconstructed from fragments of several individuals it resembled a small female gorilla), the claim that these creatures represent a link between apes and humans rests on the claims that they walked upright. Even before Johanson's find, based on fragmentary evidence, it has been the consensus of evolutionists that the australopithecines walked upright. This consensus has not gone unchallenged, however. A study of australopithecine fossils spanning 15 years with a team of scientists which rarely numbered less than four convinced Lord (Dr. Solly) Zuckerman, a famous British anatomist, that the australopithecines did not walk upright and that they are not intermediate between ape and man.[84,85]

Dr. Charles Oxnard, one of Lord Zuckerman's former students, formerly Professor of Anatomy and director of graduate studies at the University of Southern California Medical School and now at the University of Western Australia, Perth, has spent many years studying the postcranial skeleton (that part of the skeleton below the head) using the most sophisticated methods of analysis available. His studies have likewise convinced him that the australopithecines were not intermediate between ape and man and that they probably had a hanging climbing mode of locomotion similar to that of the orangutan.[86,87] Oxnard asserts that:

> . . . the australopithecines known over the last several decades from Olduvai and Sterkfontein, Kromdrai and Makapansgat, are now irrevocably removed from a place in the evolution of human bipedalism, possibly from a place in a group any closer to humans than to African apes and certainly from any place in the direct human lineage.[88]

---

[84] S. Zuckerman, *J. Roy Col. Surg. Edinburgh* 11 (1966): 87.

[85] S. Zuckerman, *Beyond the Ivory Tower* (New York: Taplinger Pub. Co., 1970), pp. 75-94.

[86] C. E. Oxnard, *American Biology Teacher* 41 (1979): 264.

[87] C. E. Oxnard, *American J. Phy. Anthro.* 52 (1980): 107.

[88] C. E. Oxnard, *The Order of Man* (New Haven: Yale University Press, New Haven, 1984), p. 332.

In his analysis Oxnard included Donald Johanson's "Lucy." Other challenges to Johanson's interpretations of the mode of locomotion of *A. afarensis* have appeared recently in the scientific literature. We conclude that the best scientific studies and analyses available demonstrate that the australopithecines neither walked erect nor had any genetic link whatsoever with humans. They are extinct apes, uniquely themselves just as are the gibbons, gorillas, chimps and orangs. If the australopithecines, the central figures in human evolutionary schemes, are eliminated from these schemes, the whole edifice is in danger of collapse.

At this point it would be well to consider the sorry record of evolutionists in their search for human ancestry. As a matter of fact, the record is so poor that Lord Zuckerman has stated that he doubted whether there was any science in this field at all.[89]

After being touted by the world's greatest authorities for nearly half a century as a sub-human ancestor, Piltdown Man was shown to be a hoax, the doctored remains of a modern ape's jaw and a recent human skull. A remarkable picture of the famous Nebraska Man, his wife and the tools they were using, all based upon a single tooth discovered in western Nebraska, was published in the *Illustrated London News* in 1922. A few years later discovery of additional remains showed that Nebraska Man was neither an ape-like man nor a man-like ape, but a pig!

For nearly a century, paleoanthropologists portrayed Neanderthal Man as a long-armed, knuckle-dragging, beetle-browed, stooped-shouldered, bow-legged, sub-human ancestor of man. It has now been established that the so-called primitive features of these creatures were due to pathological conditions such as rickets (a vitamin D deficiency), arthritis, and possibly congenital syphilis and other bone diseases. The Neanderthal creatures have now been upgraded to *Homo sapiens.*

More recently a so-called hominoid shoulder bone has been exposed as a dolphin's rib, and the skull of the so-called "Orce Man," discovered in Spain in 1983, has been shown to be that of a donkey. Another recent victim has been *Ramapithecus*, long proclaimed to be a link between man and the apes. This creature has now been shown to be essentially the same as a modern orangutan.

Lord Zuckerman was not a creationist, and thus cannot be accused of any bias towards a creationist interpretation of the evidence. Certainly Lord Zuckerman could be described as an outstanding expert in this field, having

---

[89] S. Zuckerman, *Beyond the Ivory Tower*, p. 64.

devoted many years of study in his search for man's fossil ancestry (He was first knighted, becoming Sir Solly Zuckerman, and then later was raised to the peerage, becoming Lord Zuckerman, in recognition of his distinguished scientific career). Lord Zuckerman's conclusions have been stated as follows:

> No scientist could logically dispute the proposition that man, without having been involved in any act of divine creation, evolved from some ape-like creature in a very short space of time—speaking in geological terms—without leaving any fossil traces of the steps of the transformation.[89]

In other words, what Lord Zuckerman is saying is that if the possibility of creation is excluded, obviously man must have evolved from an ape-like creature, but if he did there is certainly no evidence for it in the fossil record.

The creation scientists agree with Lord Zuckerman that there is no evidence in the fossil record that man has evolved from some ape-like creature. Thus, the fossil record, from amoeba to man, is remarkable evidence of the abrupt appearance, fully-formed, of each of the basic types of plants and animals. This is powerful positive evidence for creation.

Chapter Four

The Age of the Cosmos

Evolution would have required an immensity of time. Evolutionists reject out of hand, therefore, any evidence that suggests in any way that the earth may be recent in origin. Lord Kelvin, one of the greatest physicists of all time whose studies of a number of physical chronometers convinced him that the earth was relatively young, was referred to by Darwin as "that odious spectre." Creation scientists, some of whom believe the earth to be very old but the majority of whom believe the earth to be relatively young, urge that all of the evidence relative to the age of the earth be presented in our schools, colleges, and universities.

At the present time in our tax-supported public schools and universities, all textbooks used in these schools teach as an established fact that the earth is about 4.5 billion years old and that the universe is about 10 to 20 billion years old. Very few students become aware of the limitations of or the assumptions which are inherent in the dating methods used. Most are left to assume that it is a simple matter of counting atoms and calculating ages from these numbers. Furthermore, none of the data based on methods which indicate a young age for the earth are described.

Creation scientists urge that all of the evidence relative to the age of the cosmos be thoroughly and objectively evaluated in textbooks used in public schools, with the assumptions, limitations and practices associated with each method fully explained. Many creation scientists, for example, believe that the assumptions used in radiometric dating methods are erroneous and that such methods are used to derive assumed ages that are vastly older than the real ages. These assumptions include assumptions that decay rates have always been constant, even for billions of years, though observations

49

have extended only over a few decades and some decay rates, in fact, are known to vary; that rocks whose ages are determined have been closed systems since their formation, even in some cases for billions of years, with none of the radioisotope or the daughter product either leaving or entering the rock; and that the initial quantity of the radiometric daughter product present in the rock when it formed was either zero or that somehow, using other assumptions, its initial quantity can be derived.

It is further pointed out that when a rock is dated by several different radioactive minerals, the results are very often discordant, that is, the dates so obtained do not usually agree. Furthermore, rocks known to be young, when dated have given ages of multiplied millions of years. For example, rocks known to have formed during volcanic eruptions off the coast of Hawaii in 1800 and 1801, when dated by the potassium-argon method gave ages of 22 million years, 160 million years, and older. The explanations given by radiochronologists that argon-40 had been occluded from the environment by the rocks during their formation certainly seems valid, but how can a radiochronologist know whether or not rocks of unknown ages, which he wishes to date, had any argon in them when they first formed? He cannot. If the date obtained agrees with the date he believed to be correct to begin with, he assumes he has obtained the correct date. If the date obtained is older than the date he believes to be correct, he assumes argon has been occluded or that potassium has been leached out of the rock. If the age obtained is too young, he assumes some argon has leaked out of the rock. The pick-and-choose method widely used in radiometric dating is highly unorthodox in science.

All evolutionists, as well as some creationists, believe that in spite of the many assumptions involved in radiometric dating and in spite of the bias involved in deciding which empirically obtained dates are correct and which must be discarded as erroneous, the ages so obtained are at least approximately correct, and further, that the earth is approximately 4.5 billion years old. They also believe that, using certain cosmological theories, and assumptions, an approximate age for the universe can be obtained, although ages so obtained vary all the way from 10 billion years or less up to 20 billion years, depending upon assumptions used.

Many creation scientists, however, point to numerous physical chronometers that indicate upper limits for the ages of the earth and of the universe that are vastly younger than the assumed ages. These time clocks include those based on the amount of helium in the earth's atmosphere produced by radioactive decay of uranium and thorium,[90] the decay of the earth's magnetic field,[91] the pressure of oil in petroleum deposits,[92] the presence in rocks of pleochroic haloes of very short-lived radioisotopes,[93] the rate of cooling of the earth (taking into account heat produced by the decay of radioactive substances),[94] the Poynting-Robertson effect,[95] the lifetime of comets,[96] and the time required for clusters of galaxies to disperse,[97] just to name a few.

Creation scientists urge that all evidence supporting an old age and all evidence supporting a young age for the earth and of the universe be presented to students. The students should then be challenged to evaluate the data and to decide for themselves which view seems to be supported by the best scientific evidence. Creation scientists further point out that while establishing a young age for the earth would be fatal to evolution theory, the determination of an old age for the earth would neither be a serious blow against creation nor constitute proof of evolution. This is self-evident, since some creation scientists do accept the view that the earth is old. Furthermore, even if the age of the earth were 4.5 billion years, the time that would have been required for life to have evolved from non-life and the time required for a single-celled organism to have evolved into the complex creatures now inhabiting our planet earth would have been millions, perhaps billions, of times longer than 4.5 billion years. It is impossible to salvage evolutionary theory even with billions of years.

---

[90] M. E. Cook, *J. Colloid and Interface Sci*, 38 (1972): 18; *Nature* 50 (1957): 213.

[91] T. G. Barnes, *The Origin and Destiny of the Earth's Magnetic Field* (El Cajon, Calif.: Institute for Creation Research, 1983).

[92] M. E. Cook, *Prehistory and Earth Models* (London: Max Parrish, 1966), pp. 254—279.

[93] R. V. Gentry et al., *Nature* 252 (1974): 564; R. V. Gentry, "Radioactive Haloes," *Ann. Rev. of Nc. Sci.*, Vol. 23 (1973). See also "Time: In Full Measure," *EOS Transactions, American Geophysical Union* 60 (1979): 22.

[94] H. S. Slusher and T. P. Gamwell, *The Age of the Earth* (El Cajon, Calif.: Institute for Creation Research, 1978).

[95] H. S. Slusher and S. J. Robertson, *The Age of the Solar System* (El Cajon, Calif.: Institute for Creation Research, 1982).

[96] H. S. Slusher, *Age of the Cosmos* (El Cajon, Calif.: Institute for Creation Research, 1980), pp. 43-53.

[97] *Ibid.*, pp. 7-14.

Chapter Five

Interpreting Earth History

There is little, if any, differences in the methods employed by creation-ist geologists and evolutionist geologists in their study and application of stratigraphy, petrology, mineralogy, seismology, volcanology, and related sciences. These studies have to do with the here and now—what actually exists underfoot. The creationists and evolutionists often part company, how-ever, when attempts are made to imagine the *history* of geological formations and of the earth in general.

Up until about 1800 most geologists assumed that all major geological formations had resulted from a world-wide flood, prominently described in Hebrew literature, particularly the Bible, as well as independently in the lit-erature and legends of many peoples scattered all around the world. About that time, beginning first with the theories of James Hutton and later with those of Charles Lyell, both Englishmen, a revolution in geological thinking occurred. Hutton and Lyell insisted that, for all practical purposes, catastro-phes must be excluded as an explanation for the origin of geological forma-tions. Certainly, consideration of any world-wide catastrophe was to be completely eliminated. They contended that the present is the key to the past. Present processes, acting approximately at present rates were sufficient, given enough time, to account for all geological formations, according to Hutton and Lyell. The descriptive term, "uniformitarianism," has been widely applied to these notions. This general concept has more or less domi-nated the thinking and theorizing of geologists during the last century and a half.

Early in the nineteenth century, due largely to the studies of a number of English geologists, a so-called "geologic column" was constructed. Based upon superposition of geologic strata in local areas, and correlation, or assumed correlation, with geological strata in other areas in England, Europe, and eventually on other continents, geological strata were arranged in a sequence, beginning with the lowermost strata. The correlation was determined by the sequence in rock types and the types of fossils found in each strata.

As described earlier, a great variety of complex invertebrates are found in rocks which have been designated as belonging to Cambrian strata. Recently, fossils of fishes, which are vertebrates, have also been found in rocks of the Cambrian, although they are found more abundantly in rocks of the overlying Ordovician strata. Silurian strata generally overlie the Ordovician, and Devonian strata ordinarily overlie the Silurian. Amphibia are found abundantly in rocks of the Devonian strata. Fossils of reptiles are found in Pennsylvanian strata which are part of the Carboniferous group which generally overlies the Devonian strata. Mammals and birds occur in strata higher yet in the geologic column, with man appearing in the highest strata.

Evolutionists portray the geologic column as virtual proof of evolution.[98] Evolutionist-geologist, David Raup, points out the erroneous nature of this claim, however.[99] The theoretical construction of the geologic column was complete by 1830, thirty years before Darwin published his book. Furthermore, most of the geologists responsible for its construction were creationists! Indeed, the evidence for evolution cannot rest upon any particular sequence of organisms but must be derived from proof that all organisms have arisen from common ancestors by a process of gradual change. As we have shown earlier, the evidence is decisively contradictory to this notion. Any sequence that may be imagined from the geologic column is no more proof of evolution than the sequence—buggy—Model T Ford—Model A Ford—V-8 Ford—Modern Ford—demonstrates that a buggy evolved into a modern Ford automobile via several intermediates.

How is earth history to be interpreted in light of the geologic column? First of all, both creationist and evolutionist geologists agree that, based upon the "law of superposition," strata which underlie other strata were deposited before the overlying strata were deposited. In fact, while creationists hold consistently to this "law," evolutionists readily abandon this concept where supposedly older fossils overlie those that are supposedly younger. There are literally hundreds of places around the world where fossils occur in the wrong order for evolution, that is, where "older" fossils overlie "younger" fossils. Evolutionists maintain that in every such case faulting and

---

[98] R. Root-Bernstein, *Science* 212 (1981): 1446.
[99] D.M. Raup, *Science* 213 (1981): 298.

overthrusting has occurred in such a way that strata have been first uplifted and then thrust over adjacent strata. Subsequent erosion then eroded much of this overthrust strata, removing the upper strata with their "younger" fossils and leaving the lower, "older" fossils sitting on top of "younger" fossils which occupy the upper levels of the strata over which the adjacent strata had been thrust.

Some creationist geologists point out that while there are localized areas which show definite evidence of overthrusting, there are other areas where alleged overthrusting has occurred as evidenced by "younger" fossils underlying "older" fossils, yet there is little, if any, physical evidence that an overthrust has actually occurred. They point out, furthermore, that it is highly improbable, if not impossible, for vast blocks of strata, which sometimes include thousands of square miles, to be uplifted and thrust many miles over adjacent strata without suffering complete break up. The strata, they maintain, must have therefore been deposited in exactly the sequence found.

Whatever difficulties the standard interpretation of the geologic column entails, and they are many, advocates of this interpretation maintain that the strata of the column were laid down gradually and successively over many hundreds of millions of years. The geological formations which the creationist geologists of the early nineteenth century termed the Cambrian, Ordovician, Silurian, Devonian, etc., became geological "periods," such as the "Cambrian Period," etc. Further, these geologic "periods" have been grouped into eras—the "Paleozoic Era," the "Mesozoic Era," and the "Cenozoic Era." Each geologic period and era has been assigned an approximate time span, the Cambrian period, for example, supposedly beginning about 520 million years ago and ending about 500 million years ago, plus or minus a few million years. This view has been accepted by practically all evolutionists (there have been a few exceptions, such as Immanuel Velikovsky) and by progressive creationists.

Up until the last decade or so, evolutionist geologists, laboring under the dogma of Lyellian uniformitarian geology, have neglected or outright rejected the possibility that catastrophes have played an important role in shaping geological formations. In recent years, however, not only have creationist geologists reemphasized the importance of catastrophes in earth history,[100,101,102] but some evolutionist geologists have asserted that most

---

[100] J. C. Whitcomb and H. M. Morris, *The Genesis Flood* (Nutley, N.J.: Presbyterian and Reformed Pub. Co. 1961).

[101] S. A. Austin, *Compass* 56 (1979): 29-45.

[102] S. A. Austin, *Catastrophes in Earth History* (El Cajon, Calif.:

geological formations were formed rapidly and catastrophically.[103] As a matter of fact, some evolutionists have even become bold enough to suggest world-wide catastrophes, an absolute anathema in geological circles ever since Lyell. For example, the idea that the extinction of the dinosaurs (and of most other reptiles existing at that time) was caused by an asteroid striking the earth, creating a world-wide catastrophe,[104] has been widely discussed. Even more recently, geologists have suggested a regular recurrence of world-wide catastrophes approximately every 26 million years due to some unknown celestial cause.[105] Evolutionist Immanuel Velikovsky has become widely known for his suggestions concerning world-wide catastrophes.[106]

There is no question but that Lyellian uniformitarian dogma has been stifling to geological research just as the Darwinian dogma has been stifling to progress in biology and medicine. Creationists therefore heartily welcome the crumbling of the Lyellian dogma and a return to the recognition that catastrophes have played a leading role in earth history. Many evolutionists recognize the aid this shift lends the creationist cause and are recommending that the term "catastrophe" be avoided. It is recommended instead that it be said that earth history has been "episodic." Clever terminology, however, will not hide the fact that catastrophes, particularly world-wide catastrophes, have in fact been catastrophic.

Many creationists believe that the sediments that make up the geologic column were not laid down slowly and gradually over hundreds of millions of years but were eroded and deposited rapidly and catastrophically during a world-wide flood. They point out that if it be assumed that geological strata were eroded and deposited rapidly, vast ages for geological time can only be obtained by inserting long unseen imaginary time spans between periods of erosion and deposition.

It should be emphasized once again that the occurrence of such a flood is not only recorded in Hebrew literature, but is also described in the literature and legends of peoples all over the world, including that of Babylonia, China, South American Indians, North American Indians and many, many others.

Institute for Creation Research, 1984).

[103] Derek Ager, *The Nature of the Stratigraphic Record*, New York: Wiley, 1973.

[104] L. W. Alvarez et al., *Science* 208 (1980): 1095.

[105] S. J. Gould, *Natural History* 93 (1984): 20.

[106] I. Velikovsky, *Earth in Upheaval* (New York: Dell Pub. Co., 1955).

While it would be virtually impossible to prove beyond doubt that such an event was world-wide, the existence of the Colorado Plateau, strata approximately a mile in depth and 250,000 square miles in extent; the Tibetan Plateau, composed of sedimentary strata resting horizontally with a mean elevation of almost three miles and 750,000 square miles in extent; and continent-wide limestones, shales and sandstones and other water laid sedimentary deposits covering vast areas in many places around the world do provide evidence of a vast aqueous catastrophe.

Furthermore, under usual conditions, when an animal or plant dies and lies on the ground or either floats in the water or lies on the sea bottom, all of the remains rapidly disappear due to scavengers, bacterial decomposition, oxidation and other chemical processes or other deteriorative forces. Nothing remains, and thus no fossil forms. Fossilization occurs only when the plant or animal is rapidly buried, or much more rarely when the organism is preserved by freezing or by chemical preservation, as occurred at the La Brea tarpits. Under the usual assumptions of uniformitarian geology, therefore, we should expect to find relatively few fossils, even though life had existed on the earth for many millions of years. Actually, uncountable numbers of marine fossils exist, and billions times billions (and perhaps times billions once more) of fossils of complex marine invertebrate macrofossils are entombed in rocks formed from water-borne sediments. Vast fossil graveyards of marine and terrestrial vertebrates as well exist in many places around the world.[100] It is difficult to imagine how any combination of conditions now operating on this earth could ever account for the erosion and deposition of hundreds of thousands of square miles of sediment and the catastrophic burial and fossilization of uncountable numbers of organisms, both invertebrate and vertebrate, as well as the catastrophic burial of sufficient quantities of organisms and plant material to account for the origin of the billions of tons of oil and coal that exist upon the earth.

We can thus say that there is undoubted evidence that catastrophes have played a leading role in shaping geological formations during earth history. Furthermore, there is considerable evidence to support the possibility that this earth was at one time stricken with a flood of vast extent, even world-wide in effect. If so, then a complete re-thinking of geological history on this earth would be required. Thus, some creation scientists have suggested that the general sequence in which fossils are found in geological strata can be explained as the result of a vast world-wide aqueous catastrophe, taking into account the combination of many factors such as ecological zones, geographical distribution, mobility, hydrodynamic sorting, etc.[100]

Finally, it may be pointed out that while most geologists argue that there is no possibility that a world-wide flood ever occurred on the earth, the possibility that vast flooding was responsible for many of the major geological formations on Mars has been widely discussed in the geological literature. Yet, while here on earth we have almost 350 million cubic miles of water, sufficient to cover the entire earth to a depth of nearly two miles if the surface were smooth, Mars does not have one single drop of liquid water! The deeply embedded bias that pervades the thinking of evolutionary geologists is evident.

Chapter Six

The Legal Aspects of Teaching Creation Science

A final question remains. In view of the decision of the United States Supreme Court, by a vote of 7-2, that the Louisiana "Balanced Treatment for Creation-Science and Evolution-Science in Public School Instruction" Act violated the Establishment Clause of the First Amendment,[107] can creation-science be taught in the public schools in the United States? The answer to that question is an emphatic "Yes." The decision of the Court was not directed against teaching creation-science per se, but against the particular wording of the Act, its perceived "religious" motive, and the motives of the legislators involved in its enactment (it passed by overwhelming votes in both the senate and assembly of the Louisiana legislature). The majority opinion of the Court stated that: "The Act does not grant teachers a flexibility that they did not already possess to supplant the present science curriculum with the presentation of theories, besides evolution, about the origin of life" (p. 8). Teachers are "free to teach any and all facets of this subject" of "all scientific theories about the origin of humankind" (p. 9). "Teaching a variety of scientific theories about the origins of humankind to school children might be validly done with the clear secular intent of enhancing the effectiveness of science education" (p. 14). That this decision of the Supreme Court concerning the Louisiana law did not prohibit the teaching of creation-science in public schools has been explicitly stated by leading evolutionists following the Supreme Court decision. We cite just four examples. Harvard

---

[107] Supreme Court of the United States. No. 85-1513. Edwin W. Edwards, etc., et al. Appellants v. Don Aguillard, et al. (June 19, 1987).

professor and leading spokesman for evolution theory Stephen Jay Gould states,

> Creationists claim that their law broadened the freedom of teachers by permitting the introduction of controversial material. But no statute exists in any state to bar instruction in "creation science." It could be taught before, and it can be taught now.[108]

Evolutionary biologist Michael Zimmerman says,

> The Supreme Court ruling did not, in any way, outlaw the teaching of "creation science" in public school classrooms. Quite simply it ruled that, in the form taken by the Louisiana law, it is unconstitutional to demand equal time for this particular subject. "Creation science" can still be brought into science classrooms if and when teachers and administrators feel that it is appropriate. Numerous surveys have shown that teachers and administrators favor just this route. And, in fact, "creation science" is currently being taught in science courses throughout the country.[109]

Eugenie Scott, Director of the National Center for Science Education, the sole goal of this organization being the total suppression of teaching creation-science, stated,

> The Supreme Court decision says only that the Louisiana law violates the constitutional separation of church and state: it does not say that no one can teach scientific creationism—and unfortunately many individual teachers do. Some school districts even require "equal time" for creation and evolution.[110]

---

[108] Stephen Jay Gould, "The Verdict on Creationism," *New York Times Magazine* (July 19, 1987), p. 34.

[109] Michael Zimmerman, "Keep Guard Up After Evolution Victory," *BioScience* 37 (9, October 1987): 636.

[110] Eugenie Scott, *Nature* 329 (1987): 282.

Thus, evolutionists themselves have clearly stated that no provision of the U.S. Constitution nor any law in any state prohibits the teaching of creation-science in public schools.

William Provine, a self-professed atheist[111] and professor at Cornell University in the Section of Ecology and Systematics and Department of History, states,

> Teachers and school boards in public schools are already free under the Constitution of the USA to teach about supernatural origins if they wish in their science classes. Laws can be passed in most countries of the world requiring discussion of supernatural origins in science classes, and still satisfy national legal requirements.
>
> And I have a suggestion for evolutionists. Include discussion of supernatural origins in your classes, and promote discussion of them in public and other schools. Come off your high horse about having only evolution taught in science classes. The exclusionism you promote is painfully self-serving and smacks of elitism. Why are you afraid of confronting the supernatural creationism believed by the majority of persons in the USA and perhaps worldwide? Shouldn't students be encouraged to express their beliefs about origins in a class discussing origins by evolution?[112]

There are thus no legal, pedagogical, or scientific reasons for excluding the teaching of creation-science in public schools. Having generated fragile towers of hypotheses piled on hypotheses where fact and fiction intermingle in inextricable confusion, evolutionists apparently are fearful of allowing students to be exposed to the scientific evidence supporting creation. Evolutionists consider themselves to be the intellectual elite, sole possessors of truth, whose misguided duty is to indoctrinate students in evolutionary theory while protecting them from error.

---

[111] George Liles, "The Faith of An Atheist," *MD* (March 1994), pp. 59-64.

[112] William B. Provine, *Biology and Philosophy* 8 (1993): 124.

Chapter Seven

Summary

There is a vast body of well-established scientific evidence that supports creation while exposing fallacies and weaknesses in evolution theory. Thus creation of the universe and of its living inhabitants by the direct volitional acts of a Creator independent of and external to the natural universe is not only a credible explanation for our origin but is an explanation that is far superior to the notion that the universe created itself naturally and that life arose spontaneously on this planet.

It is unconscionable in the tax-supported public schools of our pluralistic democratic society to indoctrinate our young people in evolutionary theory while denying them the opportunity to even consider the scientific evidence for creation that thousands of scientists have found to be compelling. This results in a denial of academic and religious freedoms, indoctrination in a materialistic, mechanistic philosophy that encourages belief in atheism and agnosticism, and is poor science and poor education. The stifling stranglehold that Darwinism has exerted over our educational system must be loosened, and both the creation model and the evolution model of origins must be taught in a philosophically and religiously neutral manner.

Index of Authors

Subject Index

67

Suggestions for Further Reading

Suitable for Use in Public Schools

1. Henry Morris and Gary Parker. *What is Creation Science?* Colorado Springs, Colo.: Master Books, 2nd ed., 1987.
2. Michael Denton. *Evolution: A Theory in Crisis.* London: Burdett Books, 1985 (available from Woodbine and Associates, 6510 Belle Mill Road, Bethesda, MD 20817).
3. Soren Lovtrup. *Darwinism: The Refutation of a Myth.* New York: Croon Helm, 1987.
4. Percival Davis and Dean Kenyon. *Of Pandas and People.* Dallas: Haughton Publishing Co., 1989.
5. Charles Thaxton, Walter Bradley, and Roger Olsen. *The Mystery Life's Origin.* New York: Philosophical Library, 1984 (available from Lewis and Stanley, 13612 Midway Road, Dallas, TX 75244).
6. Francis Hitching. *The Neck of the Giraffe.* New York: Tichnor and Fields, 1982.
7. Norman Macbeth. *Darwin Retried.* Boston: Gambit, Inc., 1971.
8. Phillip E. Johnson. *Darwin on Trial.* Downer's Grove: Intervarsity Press, 1993.
9. Sir Fred Hoyle and Chandra Wickramasinghe. *Evolution in Space.* New York: Simon and Schuster, 1982.

Suitable for Private Schools and General Public

1. Henry Morris. *Scientific Creationism*, 2nd ed. Colorado Springs: Master Books, 1985.
2. Steven Austin. *Grand Canyon—Monument to Catastrophe.* El Cajon, Calif.: Institute for Creation Research, 1994.

3. Duane Gish. *Evolution: Challenge of the Fossil Record.* Colorado Springs: Master Books, 1985.
4. Duane Gish. *The Amazing Story of Creation.* El Cajon, Calif.: Institute for Creation Research, 1990.
5. Duane Gish. *Dinosaurs by Design.* Colorado Springs: Master Books, 1992.
6. John Whitcomb and Henry Morris. *The Genesis Flood.* Philadelphia: The Presbyterian and Reformed Publishing Co., 1964.
7. Malcolm Bowden. *Ape-Men: Fact or Fallacy.* Bromley, Kent, England: Sovereign Publications, 1977.
8. Lane Lester and Raymond Bohlin. *The Natural Limits to Biological Change.* Grand Rapids, Mich.:Zondervan, 1984.
9. Ian Taylor. *In the Minds of Men: Darwin and the New World Order.* Toronto: TFE Publications, 1984.
10. A.E. Wilder-Smith. *The Natural Sciences Know Nothing of Evolution,* Colorado Springs: Master Books, 1981.
11. Malcolm Bowden. *The Rise of the Evolution Fraud.* Colorado Springs: Master Books, 1982.
12. Donald Chittick. *The Controversy: The Roots of the Creation-Evolution Conflict.* Portland: Multnomah Press, 1984.
13. Henry Morris. *History of Modern Creationism.* Colorado Springs: Master Books, 1984.
14. Marvin Lubenow, *Bones of Contention.* Grand Rapids, Mich.:Baker Book House, 1992.
15. Richard B. Bliss. *Voyage to the Planets.* El Cajon, Calif.: Institute for Creation Research, 1994.
16. Richard B. Bliss. *Voyage to the Stars.* El Cajon, Calif.: Institute for Creation Research, 1991.
17. Richard B. Bliss. *Origins: Creation or Evolution.* Colorado Springs: Master Books, 1988
18. Richard B. Bliss, Duane T. Gish, and Gary Parker. *Fossils: Key to the Present.* Colorado Springs: Creation-Life Publishers, 1980.
19. Richard B. Bliss, Gary Parker and Duane Gish. *Origin of Life.* Colorado Springs: Creation-Life Publishers, 1990.